Historical Research on Social Mobility

Western Europe and the USA in the Nineteenth and
Twentieth Centuries

HARTMUT KAELBLE
Translated by Ingrid Noakes

New York Columbia University Press 1981

Library of Congress Cataloging in Publication Data

Kaeible, Hartmut.
     Historical research on social mobility.

     Translation of Historische Mobilitätsforschung.
     Bibliography: p. 137
     Includes index.
     1. Social mobility – Europe – History.
2. Occupational mobility – Europe – History.
3. Social mobility – United States – History.
4. Occupational mobility – United States – History.
I. Title.
HT609.K2713   305.5'094   80-26292
ISBN 0-231-05274-X

CONTENTS

HT
609
·K 2713

TABLES

ACKNOWLEDGEMENTS

This research report was written under the excellent working conditions provided by the West European Studies Centre at St Antony's College, Oxford. I am grateful for helpful criticism derived from discussions with historians at the Centre, with participants at a *table ronde* at the Maison des Sciences de L'Homme in Paris in 1975 and with colleagues of the Berlin Research Group for Research on the History of Modernization. I am grateful for technical help to Frau Siesslack, Frau Russau and Herr Spode. This research report originated as part of the research programme 'History of Modernization' of the Institute for Economic and Social History of the 'Zentralinstitut für sozialwissenschaftliche Forschung' at the Free University in West Berlin. The German version of the book was finished in 1977. Publications which appeared thereafter are referred to in the notes and, more comprehensively, in the bibliography.

1 INTRODUCTION

In recent years there has been a remarkable increase in research on social mobility in the nineteenth and twentieth centuries. There have been articles, debates and even whole issues devoted to it in the important social science journals. It has been the main or exclusive topic of a number of specialist conferences. Professional historians have taken up the subject for the first time. The history of social mobility is in the process of becoming a standard topic of social history. For this reason, it appears worthwhile to summarise the issues being discussed in this field — discussions which are taking place in a wide variety of disciplines — in order to make this research more accessible to social historians. Moreover, since historical research on social mobility in almost every country has developed along different lines and without much exchange of ideas, it appears necessary to report on as many countries as possible.[1]

The growth of interest in research on social mobility in history emerged out of a complex of particular issues under discussion in the social sciences, innovations in methodology and political motivations. There appear to be five main reasons why social scientists and, in particular, sociologists and historians are investigating the history of social mobility to a greater extent than hitherto. We shall indicate these reasons briefly before dealing with them in more detail later on.

1. The discussion about the relationship between industrialisation and social mobility. Modernisation and industrialisation theories often assume that industrialisation and economic development necessarily lead to greater social mobility because of a fundamental change in the structure of employment and the growing complexity of the division of labour, because of the removal of important pre-industrial obstacles to geographical and occupational mobility and because of a change in attitudes towards social mobility. The core of this argument — the higher level of mobility in modern industrial societies compared with traditional agrarian societies — has been very rarely disputed at a theoretical level. Two fields of empirical research have been developed, however, both in the USA and in Europe, in which this link has been examined and, in part, considerably modified: on the one hand, the

9

number of works by historians on social mobility in the industrial revolution has rapidly increased during the past decade and, on the other hand, the sociological debate about the trend of social mobility in the twentieth century has kept recurring since the immediate postwar period. Discussion is still continuing in both these fields.

2. The relationship between social mobility and political behaviour. At first glance, this appears to be a marginal issue and yet it was responsible for provoking historical interest in social mobility and has produced extremely stimulating work of seminal importance for the field. Again and again, historians and sociologists have been fascinated by the question whether revolutionary political consciousness depended on opportunities for social mobility, whether a revolutionary situation emerged in France at the end of the eighteenth century because the bourgeoisie only possessed limited opportunities for upward mobility into top political and social positions and, above all, whether socialist movements were more successful in Europe than in the United States because the opportunities for upward mobility were fewer for European workers and the prospects of escaping proletarian conditions of life and work very much worse. Prompted by this question, a number of case studies on the situation of American and German workers during the nineteenth century have appeared, particularly in the last few years. Nevertheless, the question of whether barriers to social mobility have really influenced class consciousness remains an open one.

3. The problem of inequality of opportunity and its origins. In contrast to the other issues mentioned so far, this is a new topic and has been strongly influenced by the political conflicts of the 1960s and early 1970s in the USA and Europe. Several emphases have emerged hitherto in characteristically different ways. One focus for research is the development of opportunities for employment and upward mobility among ethnic and cultural minorities. Although this topic would also be relevant to Europe — for example to the Polish, Italian and Jewish sections of the population in Germany — historical research has been confined almost entirely to the opportunities for mobility among minorities in the USA. One of the main reasons for this is certainly the fact that political conflicts over equal opportunities for minorities have hitherto been much sharper in the present-day USA than in Europe. Another focus for research is equality of opportunity in the education sector, above all the distribution of opportunities between social classes and groups in secondary and higher education. By contrast, this topic has been much more intensively researched for European history than for that of the USA – evidently because there is far greater inequality of educational opportunities in European secondary and higher education. Moreover, equality of opportunity in the education sector is one of the few areas in which political causes, i.e. political decisions and structures, have been researched in greater depth in the study of social mobility in history. Overall, there are more gaps in the research into the history of equality of opportunity since the industrial revolution than there are solid results. This is particularly true of the distribution of educational opportunities between social groups and classes in the USA, of the opportunities for social mobility among European ethnic and national minorities and also, in general, of equality of opportunity for women and regional minorities.

4. *The debate concerning the effects on social mobility of tendencies towards the growth of oligarchy and bureaucratisation, and in particular concerning changes in the methods of recruitment of businessmen and politicians.* Studies on the recruitment of the political elite have often been based on the continuing discussion about the decline of the notable *Honoratorien* and the emergence of the professional politicians, and about the growth of oligarchy within political parties and organisations – a discussion which goes back to Max Weber and Robert Michels. This raised the question of how far modern political structures facilitated upward movement from the middle and lower classes or how far the political elite increasingly shut itself off and recruited from its own ranks. Studies of the recruitment of the economic elite often took their starting point from the emergence of large firms and the bureaucratisation of the private sector and examined whether these processes were leading to a growing formalisation of the careers of the business elite, to the end of the classic Self-Made Man, and to an exclusive economic elite. These are both topics of research in the field of social mobility in history which have been frequently covered – and not simply in recent years. Characteristically, the research on the USA has concentrated in particular on the recruitment of the business elite, the research on Europe on the origins of the political elite. There is no unanimity about the long-term historical trend in recruitment either in the field of research on political elites or in that on businessmen.

5. *The use of quantitative methods in historical research.* Alongside the history of population, urbanisation, social protest and elections, the

history of social mobility has become one of the most important fields in social history for the use of quantitative methods. A large number of studies have proved that the history of social mobility can only be reliably written with the help of quantification methods and, moreover, that quantitative analysis is more appropriate to some of the factors conditioning it. Arguments based on representative quantitative evidence have replaced speculations about particular instances which may be striking but are usually untypical. It was certainly an advance for quantitative methods to be assessed not simply in terms of merely playing with numbers, of the short-sighted neglect of non-quantifiable factors and processes, or of the esoteric discussions about indicators and techniques which were initially necessary. However, the best works on social mobility in history have never confined themselves to the use of quantitative methods. Such methods have only proved themselves more productive, more precise and more convincing when they have been combined with qualitative methods, and when they were not used as ends in themselves, but as means for the development of original theories and the achievement of new insights.

These topics have not only stimulated research in the history of social mobility in modern industrial society; they have also had the reverse effect that in all the countries dealt with here there have been very few studies of the history of income mobility, of mobility in the agrarian sector, of the recruitment of white-collar workers, of the *petite bourgeoisie* – and this is largely true also of the upper middle class, of the practice of promotion in various occupations and the distribution of opportunities in the spheres of business and the bureaucracy, and of the multifaceted role of government and the administration. These subjects, therefore, can only be dealt with cursorily here. The following account will also only deal with geographical mobility in a peripheral way since this topic can be outlined more effectively in connexion with demographic history or the history of urbanisation and is, in fact, usually researched in this context. Moreover, this report will concentrate primarily on the USA, France, Great Britain and Germany, and because of language barriers will unfortunately remain patchy for certain countries in which social mobility has also been investigated such as the Netherlands, Sweden, Poland and Denmark. Furthermore, the account will restrict itself to developments since the industrial revolution. For this reason, excellent studies of social mobility such as those by Lawrence Stone, Emmanuel Le Roy Ladurie, and Karl Bosl will not be considered. For, in view of the limited size of this volume, a longer timespan would have resulted in excessively superficial information. Finally, this report will not — as originally planned — deal with historical research on social stratification and social inequality, although that would have been very useful, since many of the debates on social mobility lead on to questions of class and social inequality. But this too would have gone beyond the limits of this brief book.[2]

The structure of this research report is dictated by the focal points of historical research on social mobility. To start with, the studies of the long-term trend of social mobility and its relationship to industrialisation are introduced. These studies usually deal with the whole society of a city or a country. Thereafter follow chapters on particular aspects: historical research on the opportunities for occupational and upward mobility on the part of industrial workers is summed up in the third chapter; the fourth chapter provides a synopsis of historical studies on the inequality of opportunity in the educational sector, above all in secondary and university education; the fifth chapter deals with the recruitment of businessmen and of political elites; the final chapter aims to provide information on the most important concepts and methods. In general, the report focuses on analyses of the long-term historical change in social mobility. This main theme forms the context in which the particular research studies are introduced and within which the basic controversies, conclusions and gaps in our knowledge are described. In this way, an attempt is made not only to provide a synopsis of the state of research but at the same time to offer suggestions for future research.[3]

2 THE TREND OF SOCIAL MOBILITY

There has been a very lively and extended controversy among historians of social mobility about the question of its long-term development: on the one hand, in terms of society as a whole, which will be dealt with in this section and, on the other hand, from the point of view of particular social strata, classes, occupational and educational groups, which we shall return to selectively later on. As far as the consideration of the totality of society is concerned, superficially the discussion focuses on the question of whether the rates of social mobility in the nineteenth and twentieth centuries increased, stagnated or decreased. In the background, however, there are almost always contradictory views about industrialisation and its effects on social mobility. Many social scientists are of the opinion that industrialisation inevitably produces a more open, mobile, achievement-oriented society, since economic growth is impossible without a continuous process of change in the occupational structure and, therefore, without a high level of occupational mobility. Social scientists who hold this view expect social mobility to increase rapidly in modern industrial society or at any rate to be at a high level. Another group, however, holds that industrialisation and low rates of social mobility are entirely compatible and that, therefore, numerous political and cultural barriers remain, or can even develop in modern industrial society, which hinder social mobility. According to this view, state intervention and changes in social values acquire considerable significance for the development of social mobility. A third school of thought views the theories concerning the effects both of industrialisation and political intervention in West European and North American societies with extreme scepticism; it regards obstacles and barriers to social mobility as laws of capitalist society, which cannot be removed without changing the relations of production, or else sees social mobility primarily as an instrument of repression and corruption with the function of stabilising capitalist society. Among these schools of thought two historical debates have emerged over the years with varying participants. These debates deal with the transitional society of industrialisation on the one hand, and with the industrial society of the twentieth century on the other. Both of them are conducted so independently of one another that it is preferable to consider them separately.

Industrialisation

The industrial revolution is regarded by the overwhelming majority of social scientists as a period in which social mobility rapidly increased. Despite very varying estimations, they argue that occupational change and migration, i.e., the emergence of the working class and of industrialists, the decline of the peasantry and the *petite bourgeoisie*, the transatlantic migration of Europeans and the flight from the countryside in the USA and Europe during the industrial revolution, led to an enormous increase in occupational mobility. Many social scientists consider this revolution in the occupational structure a unique event in European and North American history and believe, therefore, that never before or since were the rates of social mobility so high nor have they increased so rapidly as during the industrial revolution. Up to now this view has seldom been systematically investigated. It is true that there are a considerable number of empirical studies. In the first place, however, they are organised in a very disparate manner, using differing methods to cover cities, regions, or countries. Secondly, they are primarily descriptions of the trend of mobility. Hitherto there has not been a thorough discussion of the conditions for and the causes of social mobility during the industrial revolution. Nevertheless, some preliminary conclusions can already be drawn from these studies.

Several empirical studies support the idea of the unique development of social mobility during the industrial revolution. Retrospective studies which cover very long timespans of the modern history of industrialised countries almost invariably show sharply rising rates of social mobility for the more distant past. Guy Pourcher demonstrated this in his study of France – which was excellently structured from a historical point of view although based on a small sample – as did Gerhard Kleining in two of the most comprehensive, though somewhat controversial, studies of social mobility in Germany. John C. Goyder and James E. Curtis have put forward similar theories for the USA and Gösta Carlsson for Sweden.[1] Several urban studies point in the same direction, studies which are not based on retrospective sociological methods but on historical sources (and for this reason are susceptible to more precise historical categorisation, as will be shown in the last chapter). In his study of the social history of Rotterdam, Henk van Dijk came to the conclusion that intragenerational upward mobility increased above all in the 1870s, whereas downward mobility showed no clear-cut trend. Van Dijk explains this development in terms of an intensification of the economic relations between Rotterdam and Britain and with the

Table 2.1: The trend of social mobility in Europe and the USA in the nineteenth and twentieth centuries*

Germany/Federal Republic		France		Sweden		England & Wales		USA	
Year of birth	Proportion of those mobile	Year of birth	Proportion of those mobile	Year of birth	Proportion of those mobile	Year of birth	Proportion of those mobile	Year of birth	Proportion of those mobile
(1)	(2)	(3)	(4)	(5)	(6)	(7)	(8)	(9)	(10)
1888-1890	21	1850-1879	46						
1891-1895	38	1880-1889	46			-1890	67		
1896-1900	34	1890-1899	48			1890-1899	64		
1901-1905	50	1900-1909	49	1899-1905	32	1900-1909	66	1898-1907	78
1906-1910	48			1908-1914	31	1910-1919	64	1908-1917	80
		1910-1919	53	1917-1923	29	1920-1929	63	1918-1927	80
		1920-1929	55					1928-1937	80

*This table is only intended to provide a comparison of the trends. The rates of social mobility cannot be compared since the criteria used for the surveys are too varied. Moreover, in the case of France it is concerned with intragenerational mobility and not as in the other cases with inter-generational mobility.

Source: For columns (1) and (2): G. Kleining, 'Soziale Mobilität in der Bundesrepublik Deutschland' II: 'Status-oder Prestigemobilität', *Kölner Zeitschrift für Soziologie und Sozialpsychologie*, 27 (1975), p. 113; cols. (3) and (4): G. Pourcher, 'Un essai d'analyse par cohorte de la mobilité géographique et professionelle en France', *Acta Sociologica*, 9, (1965), p. 147; cols. (5) *and* (6): G. Carlsson, *Social Mobility and Class Structure* (Lund, 1958), pp. 94ff; cols. (7) *and* (8): D.V. Glass & J.R. Hall, 'Social Mobility in Great Britain' in D.V. Glass (ed.) *Social Mobility in Britain*, p. 188; cols. (9) and (10): R.M. Hauser *et al.*, 'Structural Changes in Occupational Mobility Among Men in the United States', *American Socio-logical Review*, 40 (1975), p. 591.

Ruhr area, and sees in that an indirect link with industrialisation. Van Dijk, however, defines social mobility not only as a change of occupation but also as an improvement or deterioration in individual incomes. He stresses that the higher rates of mobility in the 1870s, above all among members of the working class, are dependent not so much on changes in occupation as on improvements in income. Renate Mayntz established in one of the rare investigations of social mobility in German cities that the occupational mobility between generations in Euskirchen, a small textile town in the Eifel, was particularly high in the 1830s. She explains this in terms of rapid economic change. In a parallel study of Cologne, Hans Jürgen Daheim came to the conclusion that the rates of intergenerational social mobility showed a particularly marked increase between the 1830s and the 1870s. He too explained the acceleration of occupational mobility in terms of the initial stages of industrialisation with the resultant 'revolutionary change in the social structure'.[2] In none of these works, however, — with the exception of van Dijk's study — is the period of local industrialisation the central topic. Thorough historical works which confirm the theory of the particularly high or increasing rates of social mobility during this period and document it with convincing empirically based arguments, are therefore still extremely rare. It is, therefore, paradoxical that for a long time this idea of intensive vertical social mobility during industrialisation has proved extremely pervasive, particularly in the USA, as a result of the influence of a study which neither contains statistical evidence nor uses historical methods: W.L. Warner's study of Newburyport (he called it Yankee City), a small industrial town in New England, one of the oldest parts of the USA, which, even during the time of Warner's fieldwork in the 1940s had not been affected by the urbanisation of the twentieth century, and which, therefore, could represent the prototype of the classic American town. In a vague and yet influential assessment, Warner stated that in Yankee City, 'upward and downward movements were continually taking place in the lives of many people'.[3]

In the past two decades, social historians in particular have produced very different assessments of social mobility during the industrial revolution. This revision of the accepted view was introduced by the pioneering work of Stephan Thernstrom on the unskilled workers of Newburyport in the nineteenth century in which he sharply attacked Warner's thesis. Thernstrom, who was one of the first historians to apply quantification methods to the history of social mobility, did not find unusually high geographical mobility; in the period under investigation – the years 1850-80 – almost the whole population who were there during the first year had moved away by the end, and almost the whole population during the final year were recent arrivals. The rates of career mobility and of intergenerational mobility, however, were disappointingly low – among immigrants and native born inhabitants alike – and did not increase during the period under investigation. Thernstrom explains this – and this is a point we shall have to return to – in terms of the specific concepts which the Newburyport workers had of upward social mobility. Other studies which deal with cases more productive for the question of the relationship between the industrial revolution and social mobility confirm this impression (see Table 2.2). Peter Knight's work on Boston between 1830 and 1860, one of the most important and expanding cities in the USA (it was simultaneously a port, a commercial centre and an immigrant centre), comes to the conclusion that there was no increase in occupational mobility, or in downward or upward mobility. Stuart Blumin's work on the port and commercial city of Philadelphia showed that from the 1830s onwards only the rates of downward mobility increased, whereas, surprisingly, upward mobility showed no tendency to increase. Blumin explains this as a consequence of the rise of large-scale production in Philadelphia which – encouraged by the revolution in transportation and the waves of Irish and German immigrants – destroyed the artisanal forms of production and thereby reduced opportunities for upward social mobility. Clyde Griffen's thorough investigation of the small town of Poughkeepsie in New York State and Michael Katz's sophisticated study of Hamilton (Canada) also confirm the impression which Thernstrom gained from the case of Newburyport.[4] In one of the rare studies of European cities, Tom Rishoy investigated the social origins of the inhabitants of Copenhagen in 1850, 1900 and 1953. In this case too, the rates of social mobility did not alter appreciably, although Copenhagen grew rapidly during the second half of the nineteenth century.[5] A whole series of studies on opportunities for upward mobility among industrial workers and on the recruitment of the business elite during the industrial revolution confirm the impression that the effects of the industrial revolution on social mobility have been overestimated. We shall return to these works later on.

The debate on the effects of the industrial revolution on social mobility has by no means been decided or concluded. Against the sceptical theory one can, above all, point out that we are still some way from knowing whether the rates of social mobility changed during the industrial revolution. So far there have only been studies of particular

Table 2.2: Occupational career mobility in North American and European cities in the nineteenth and twentieth centuries (per cent)*

	Philadelphia (1)	Boston (2)	Pough-keepsie, USA (3)	Newbury-port, USA (4)	Norristown, USA (5)	Hamilton, Canada (6)	Rotterdam (7)
1820-1830	14						
1830-1840	19	22					19
1840-1850	15	18					
1850-1860	20	23	22	36		29	21
1860-1870			19	26			
1870-1880			18	21			29
1880-1890		26					
1890-1900							
1900-1910							
1910-1920		31			24		
1920-1930					29		
1930-1940		26			34		
1940-1950					35		
1950-1960							
1960-1970		27					

*The table is intended above all to illustrate the trend; it limits itself, therefore, to historical studies which follow social mobility over a long timespan. In the individual studies occupational mobility is observed over the course of a decade (Poughkeepsie is an exception) , but between very different occupational groups.
Source: Col. 1: S. Blumin, 'Mobility and Change in Ante-Bellum Philadelphia', in S. Thernstrom & R. Sennett (eds.), *Nineteenth-Century Cities*, (New Haven, London, 1969), pp. 173ff; col. 2: P. R. Knights, *The Plain People of Boston, 1830-1860* (New York, 1971), pp. 98f (1830-1860); S. Thernstrom, *The Other Bostonians* (Cambridge, 1973), p. 53 (1880-1970); col. 3: C. Griffen, 'Making it in America: Social Mobility in Mid-Nineteenth Century Poughkeepsie', *New York History*, 51 (1970), p. 435; col. 4: Thernstrom, *Poverty and Progress*, p. 96; col. 5: S. Goldstein, *Patterns of Mobility 1910-1950: The Norristown Study* (Philadelphia, 1958), pp. 169ff; col. 6: M. Katz, *The People of Hamilton, Canada West: Family and Class in a Mid-Nineteenth Century City* (Cambridge, 1976); col. 7: H. van Dijk, *Rotterdam 1810-1880* pp. 152ff.

**Table 2.3: Occupational mobility between generations in North
American and European cities in the nineteenth and twentieth centuries
(proportion of those mobile) (per cent)**

	Boston (1)	India-napolis (2)	Hamilton (Canada) (3)	Copen-hagen (4)	Cologne (5)	Euskirchen (6)
1830						
1840					49 (52)[b]	61 (45)[b]
1850	54[a]		20[c]	39		
1860			28[c]			
1870	56[a]				56 (53)[b]	51 (44)[b]
1880	56[a]					
1890				26		
1900						
1910	51[a]	35			61 (55)[b]	55 (46)[b]
1920						
1930	52[a]					
1940		35				
1950					63 (58)[b]	64 (50)[b]
1960						
1970		37				

[a]Year of birth. [b]Converted into four groups (higher white collar, lower white
collar, skilled worker, unskilled worker) to secure rough comparability with
American results. [c]Only three groups (professional or commercial, skilled, semi-
skilled or unskilled).
Source: Col. 1: Thernstrom, *The Other Bostonians*, p. 105; col. 2: J.C. Tully,
E.F. Jackson & R.F. Curtis, 'Trends in Occupational Mobility in Indianapolis',
Social Forces, 49 (1970/71), p. 193; col. 3: Katz, *The People of Hamilton*,
p. 166; col. 4: T. Rishoy, 'Metropolitan Social Mobility', p. 136f; col. 5: Mayntz,
Industriegemeinde, pp. 154ff; col. 6: Daheim, 'Berufliche Intergenerationen-
Mobilität', pp. 117ff.

phases of industrialisation. We lack case studies which examine, in
particular, industrial cities over a sufficiently long timespan and discover how the rates of social mobility developed before, during and
after the industrial revolution. Moreover, so far research has concentrated too much on the big ports and commercial centres such as Marseilles, Cologne, Rotterdam, Boston, Philadelphia and on the less
expanding towns like Poughkeepsie, Newburyport and Euskirchen.
There is still no study on the long-term development of social mobility
in rapidly expanding industrial cities.

There are, however, several arguments to be put forward against the

theory of unusually high or rising rates of social mobility during the industrial revolution. In the first place, the speed and impact of the economic and social upheavals of the industrial revolution are generally
overestimated in this context. Processes which have undoubtedly influenced social mobility such as the reduction of the agricultural sector,
the decline of the *petite bourgeoisie*, the rapid increase in white-collar
employees and civil servants, the changes in occupational qualifications,
the process of urbanisation – were frequently in an embryonic stage
during the industrial revolution or occurred just as rapidly and with as
great an impact in the twentieth century, and with consequences which
were of equal significance. To describe the industrial revolution as a
unique 'period of social upheaval' is an exaggeration in view of the
development of the social structure in all industrial countries and is, at
most, applicable to particular industrial cities and regions. Secondly,
the two cases examined so far in Germany (Cologne and Euskirchen)
tend rather to strengthen the doubts about this theory since they certainly do not fit into the pattern of the rapidly expanding industrial
city. In Cologne, industrialisation and the transformation of the occupational structure were still in their initial stages until the 1870s and
therefore – according to the French social historian, Pierre Aycoberry
– upward social mobility was still limited. In Euskirchen, too, the
1830s are not a period of crucial changes in the economic and social
structure; the high rates of mobility are largely based on the mobility
between agricultural and non-agricultural occupations and may well be
a sign of agricultural overpopulation and not of the beginnings of
industrialisation but rather of insufficient industrialisation.[6] Thirdly,
too little research has been devoted hitherto to the effects of the
change in social differentials of birthrates, life expectancy and family
size during the nineteenth century on the development of social mobility. It is conceivable that the demographic transition hindered
upward and encouraged downward social mobility since life expectancy
among the upper social strata increased faster than among the middle
and lower strata. On the other hand, the growth in population linked
with demographic transition increased the rates of occupational
mobility.[7] Fourthly, and finally, social mobility has often been too
readily assumed on the basis of geographical mobility. The nineteenth
century was undoubtedly a period of unprecedented rates of social
mobility. Neither before nor since has there been such a high level of
transatlantic migration or such migration within North American and
European countries. There are strong reasons for assuming, however,
that this migration was largely provoked by poor career chances and

few opportunities for upward mobility. High social mobility, therefore, was probably not the consequence of these migrations, but low social mobility their cause.[8] On the whole, therefore, the present state of research reinforces doubts about the theory that the industrial revolution led to an explosive and unique increase in occupational mobility. Even if it should emerge − as expected − that occupational mobility increased in comparison with pre-industrial society, it is most probable that downward mobility predominated. Upward mobility would have been relatively low during the industrial revolution.[9]

The Twentieth Century

The debate about the development of social mobility in the twentieth century has been going on for some time; it is somewhat more complex and is based on a wider range of empirical material. There are basically three main schools of thought: one school asserts that the rates of social mobility declined, the second that they stagnated and the third that they increased. The theory of the decline in the rates of social mobility is the oldest and was often put forward in the interwar years. American sociologists, in particular, feared that the process of economic concentration, the serious economic crisis and the reduction in immigration would restrict the openness of American society.[10] However, only one example of this development has been confirmed by an empirical study and that was outside the USA: Theodor Geiger's work on the Danish port and industrial city of Aarhus. Geiger established the social origins of the inhabitants of Aarhus by posing additional questions during the Danish census of 1949. The retrospective analysis of the results showed that occupational mobility in Aarhus had decreased during the seventy years preceding the census. Geiger's results, however, remained a special case since he made his observations at the end of a long phase of low rates of economic growth, determined by war and recession, which undoubtedly also had a negative influence on social mobility.[11]

Although the theory of the decline in rates of social mobility has not proved to be correct, it has had an extremely stimulating effect and has prompted numerous empirical investigations of the historical development of social mobility. Although the first wave of such studies in the late 1940s and the 1950s disproved the theory of decline, it did, however, in the main support the scarcely more optimistic theory of the stagnation of social mobility during the twentieth century. The pioneering work by Natalie Rogoff, one of the first urban studies of social mobility to use quantification, compared the social origins of the inhabitants of the Indianapolis metropolitan area between 1910 and 1940 and discovered no increase in social mobility. The first large-scale study of social mobility in a European country, which was carried out by David Glass's group at the London School of Economics in 1949, covering England and Wales, also observed only stagnation in the decades prior to the investigation. It did, however, suggest the possibility that the English educational reforms of 1944 might manifest themselves in later studies in the form of rising rates of social mobility. In 1950-54, Gösta Carlsson examined social mobility between generations in the Swedish population (see Table 2.1). He too could not discover a firm trend towards a change in social mobility. The hitherto most comprehensive investigation of social mobility in the Netherlands, carried out by J.J.M. van Tulder in 1954, also concluded that occupational career mobility varied — as a result of disturbances in economic growth — but did not show any recognisable trend between 1919 and 1954. From the comparison of admittedly very heterogeneous analyses of the inhabitants of Copenhagen in the years 1900 and 1953-4, which has already been referred to, Tom Rishoy gained the impression that the mobility between generations did not increase in the twentieth century. Several more recent studies support the theory of the stagnation of social mobility in the twentieth century: Stephan Thernstrom, who analysed the development of inter- and intra-generational mobility in Boston between 1880 and 1970, discovered high but on the whole constant rates of social mobility (see Tables 2.2 and 2.3). Nor could Howard Chudacoff discover any trend towards rising rates of social mobility between 1880 and 1920 in his study of Omaha, a rapidly growing business and commercial centre in Nebraska. Indeed, his expectations regarding possibilities for occupational and upward mobility in a 'frontier city' were if anything disappointed in Omaha. Gerhard Kleining, who in 1969-70 undertook the hitherto most comprehensive investigation of social mobility in Germany and the Federal Republic, agreed with the stagnation theory in his interpretation of his data. In his opinion, the decisive factor was the survival of the capitalist power structure. In a review of French research, Jane Marceau put forward the thesis that despite substantial changes in the French social structure during the postwar period, inequality of opportunity neither decreased significantly nor lost any vestige of its class character. The opportunities for upward mobility among peasants and workers remained few and random; while the middle strata were often mobile, it was only over short social distances; and the upper strata were almost completely secure against social decline. In a résumé of recent research, Raymond Boudon considered it indisputable that social mobility was stagnating in industrial societies.[12]

The stagnation thesis is not, however, by any means supported by all empirical studies of social mobility. The more recent such works are, the more frequently they suggest a slight increase in social mobility. The study of Peter Blau and Otis D. Duncan, which has become a classic, analysed the historical development of social mobility in the USA up to 1962 using a variety of methods. The bulk of its results showed a slight rise in social mobility. The recent re-examination of the Blau-Duncan theory, which was carried out by a group led by Robert M. Hauser, using new methods and new data, confirmed this. Two American local studies produced similar results: Sidney Goldstein, who

Figure 2.1: Rates of occupational social mobility of men aged 20-24 in France*

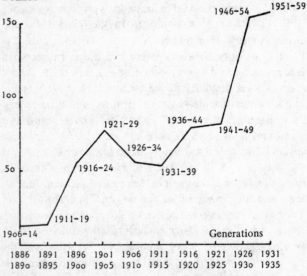

*G. Pourcher, 'Die geographische und berufliche Mobilität in Frankreich' in G. Szell (ed.), *Regionale Mobilität* (Munich, 1972), p. 222.

analysed the development of career mobility between 1910 and 1950 in Norristown, an almost static part of the Philadelphia metropolitan area, discovered a trend towards gradually rising rates of occupational mobility (see Table 2.2). The Tully-Jackson-Curtis group, which continued the Rogoff study of Indianapolis in 1967, came to the conclusion that the social origins of the inhabitants of the Indianapolis metropolitan area suggest a higher level of social mobility after the Second World War, but considered the results to be a special case.[13] The thesis of a slight increase in social mobility has also been confirmed in several studies of West European countries. A. Darbel was the first to compare the three major surveys of the post-war period in France with one another. He came to the conclusion that, between 1954 and 1970, upward mobility in France had increased, particularly in the upper ranks of business and the civil service. The best explanation for this development appeared to him to be the rapid expansion of these top-level positions. Another pre-condition for this increase can be concluded from a study carried out by Guy Pourcher in 1959, which was excellently planned, though on the basis of a rather small sample. The great advantage of his study – we will have to come back to this in the last chapter – was that it could ascertain far better than the other retrospective sociological studies when the interviewees were occupationally mobile and moving up or down. As a result, whereas most retrospective investigations can only make very tentative statements about trends, it was possible for him to develop theories about very much more short-term variations in social mobility. The rates of intra-generational occupational mobility rose sharply between the beginning of the twentieth century and the 1920s, stagnated or declined at the latest from the world economic crisis until the end of the Second World War, and after that rose again steeply until 1959. This could represent a trend towards a slight increase in social mobility in the twentieth century.[14] The thesis of a slight increase in social mobility has also been documented in studies of other European countries. Svalastoga observed rising mobility rates in a retrospective analysis of the Danish population in 1953-4. Above all, the second comprehensive investigation of social mobility in England and Wales, carried out in 1972 by Goldthorpe, concluded that upward mobility into jobs demanding high qualifications increased in the course of the twentieth century. Goldthorpe, however, did not share Glass's optimistic assumption that the decisive reason for this was greater equality of opportunity in the education sector. Like Darbel, he considered the disproportionate increase in occupations demanding high qualifications to be the decisive factor.[15]

Only in the Federal Republic of Germany was there a real debate about the question whether there was stagnation or a slight increase in social mobility in the twentieth century. It was provoked by Kleining's theory that occupational mobility and upward and downward mobility had not changed in pre-1945 Germany and the Federal Republic during the past fifty years. The sociologists, Karl Ulrich Mayer and Walter Müller, had serious doubts about Kleining's results, primarily on methodological grounds. In the first place, they argued that by using improved methods to test Kleining's data, while it was not statistically certain, it did appear possible that, during the twentieth century, mobility rates in Germany and the Federal Republic had increased slightly on a long-term basis. Secondly, their comparison of various studies of social mobility in the Federal Republic between 1956 and 1969 showed that both stagnation as well as a slight increase in inter-generational social mobility were within the bounds of possible statistical interpretation.[16] On the basis of the unusually large number of older studies of the social origins of various occupational groups in Germany, the author of this research report has estimated rates of social mobility for the last phase of Imperial Germany and for the Weimar Republic and compared them with surveys of the Federal Republic. The results point along the same lines. The rates of social mobility between the Weimar Republic and the early years of the Federal Republic clearly increased, partly because of post-war prosperity in the Federal Republic, but to a large extent, however, because of the removal of political barriers and cultural obstacles to social mobility over the long term. In this way, the mobility rates of the Federal Republic appear to have drawn closer to those of the USA and Great Britain, from which Germany had differed during the Empire and even in the Weimar Republic as a result of its more rigid and less previous social structure. In his interpretation of a second survey of 1974, Gerhard Kleining finally modified his stagnation theory fundamentally. While in principle adhering to his former line of argument, he now formed the impression that the rates of occupational mobility between generations in the Federal Republic were going up with a jump. Apart from the specifically political factors of the immediate postwar years, such as the political and economic collapse and radical change, the refugee movements and the occupational vacancies caused by loss of life during the war, he explains this increase in the mobility rates on the basis of long-term postwar economic prosperity. Regional and local analyses in the Federal Republic also point along the same lines. The studies on Euskirchen and Cologne, already referred to, show slightly increasing mobility rates between *c.* 1910 and *c.* 1950 (see Table 2.3), while at the same time, an exact date, and therefore the reasons for this increase, remain an open question. In an analysis of social mobility in Schleswig-Holstein between the Weimar Republic and the early years of the Federal Republic, Karl Martin Bolte also found increasing rates of social mobility between the generations. He, too, explained this, above all, on the basis of specific political circumstances during the postwar period, namely the movement of refugees.[17]

Summing up the research on the development of social mobility in the twentieth century, one must conclude that little has been established. The only possibilities which have been excluded are of a rapid increase in social mobility or of a decrease. It is still an open question, however, whether social mobility in the industrial society of the twentieth century stagnated or increased slightly. Certainly the stagnation thesis is no longer entirely convincing since it is contradicted by a number of points. Firstly, it was mostly put forward by studies which were produced during the immediate postwar period. Since the retrospective method usually only goes back 30 or 40 years, these studies only cover a timespan in which disturbances in economic growth may have hindered social mobility particularly seriously and which is, therefore, unsuitable for statements about long-term and general trends in industrial society. Secondly, retrospective investigations, which have nearly always been used to document the stagnation theory, have hitherto given extremely unreliable historical results because of the way in which the questionnaires have been designed. We shall have to return to this in the final chapter. Thirdly, the stagnation theory is almost always associated with the idea that the rates of social mobility in industrial societies of the twentieth century are considerably higher than in pre-industrial societies and that this high level of mobility was achieved through a sudden increase in the rates of mobility during a phase of social change caused by the industrial revolution which, in fact, never occurred in this unique and sudden form in any of the developed countries of Europe and North America. Since, on the contrary, the industrial revolution initiated a long-term phase of continuous change in the occupational and social structure which has never been interrupted, the theory of an admittedly fluctuating, but since the industrial revolution slightly increasing, rate of social mobility appears more plausible. These arguments do not completely refute the stagnation thesis. But it appears certain that this theory cannot apply either to all industrial countries or to all periods of twentieth-century industrial society. However, a research discussion as to whether the stagnation thesis or the theory of a slight increase in mobility can claim universal validity would be rather futile. It seems rather more important to decide under which conditions social mobility in industrial countries either increased or stagnated during the twentieth century.

Historical research has only just made tentative beginnings in this extremely important field. Six possible conditions have been investigated or discussed so far. They support in part the stagnation thesis and in part the theory of an increase in mobility.

The Expansion of Education and Social Mobility

One of the most popular theories of the 1960s was that education influences social mobility; that greater equality of educational opportunity leads to greater equality of occupational opportunity. This is a central issue for the historical development of social mobility in the twentieth century since academic education expanded strongly in all industrial countries during this period. The effect of this expansion of education on social mobility has, however, been assessed with growing scepticism in recent years by social scientists with an interest in history. The prevailing opinion today is that the effect on occupational opportunities was only slight. In his 1958 analysis of the development of social mobility in Sweden, Carlsson already treated this correlation with great reserve. John Ridge has recently pursued the question of why the rates of social mobility stagnated in England until at least 1949, although secondary education clearly expanded in the first half of the twentieth century. For this purpose, he used Glass's survey of 1949 to compare the educational opportunities and occupational success of an older and a younger generation with each other. In a very rare combination of quantitative and qualitative-historical analysis he came to the conclusion that in England qualifications and merit were increasingly important for occupational success, but that, at the same time, the educational standards of sons in most types of school increasingly depended on the social status of their fathers. Social mobility, therefore, tended rather to decrease. Ridge himself, however, did stress that he had been dealing with an untypical period. The education of the younger generation. especially in the lower classes, was seriously hampered by the rapidly rising cost of education during the world economic crisis of the 1930s, and by a shortage of teachers and by evacuation during the Second World War. He could not yet trace the effects of the education reform of 1944. The evaluation of a new survey by the Oxford Group on Social Mobility in which Ridge is participating should, therefore, be of great interest. Duncan and Featherman have made a similar study for the United States. They investigated in four different age cohorts the correlation between the occupation and education of fathers and the occupation, education and income of sons. They too were unable to establish a decline in the correlation between the occupation and education of fathers and sons in the course of the twentieth century. Admittedly, they did not carry out a thorough historical analysis such as that of Ridge. Finally, Boudon tried to summarise these research results in the thesis that, generally, in modern industrial societies increasing educational opportunities do not lead to higher rates of social mobility. In his view, the expansion of education only resulted in more candidates applying for positions requiring qualifications, which lowered the status, i.e. the income and prestige of these posts, so that the anticipated rise in social status did not occur at all or only to a lesser extent. In his view, a policy of increasing educational opportunity was not, therefore, an effective instrument for expanding mobility and equality of occupational opportunity.[18]

All these studies arrive at results which support the stagnation theory, and which help to explain it and make it seem more plausible. All these analyses do, however, contain more or less explicitly, two qualifications: firstly, they dealt primarily with the expansion of educational opportunities and to a lesser degree with the distribution of opportunities in the education sector. This was certainly not a mistake, since in the industrial countries of the twentieth century the distribution of opportunities in the education sector on the whole changed little, and opportunities for less favoured groups — farmers, low-ranking non-manual employees, and above all workers — improved only a little. Secondly, the sceptical assessment of the effect of the expansion in education was only valid — as Boudon above all stressed — in the event that the social structure did not change and the posts for which more candidates were trained did not multiply more quickly than other occupations. This qualification leads to the second factor of social mobility, which has been more thoroughly discussed.

Changes in the Social Structure and Social Mobility

The effect of structural change on social mobility has been discussed ever since the beginnings of historical research on mobility. Two changes in the social structure in particular led to high or rising rates of social mobility in the twentieth century: firstly, the continuing growth in the numbers of white-collar employees and civil servants. This offered major or increasing possibilities for upward mobility for those with manual occupations, provided there were no social barriers standing in the way. The majority of social scientists, however, hold the view that this process only explains the high rates of social mobility in the twentieth century; it did not lead to a long-term rise in social mobility since the expansion of occupations for white-collar employees and civil servants neither began in the twentieth century nor was the trend noticeably accelerated. The second change was the major increase in occupations requiring high qualifications, which only began in the twentieth century in most industrial countries, and is generally regarded as the most important effect of the current scientific and technical revolution on the social structure. In his investigation of social mobility in England and Wales, John Goldthorpe took the view that this is the decisive reason for the increase in upward mobility in the twentieth century. In his comparison of surveys of social mobility in France carried out in the past twenty years, A. Darbel also came to the conclusion that this change in the social structure provides the most plausible explanation for the increase in upward mobility. Peter M. Blau and Otis D. Duncan are also of the opinion that the increase in professional and semi-professional occupational groups in the twentieth century generally has led to and will continue to lead to increasing upward mobility in industrial societies.[19] This is the decisive and best-documented argument for the theory of a slight increase in social mobility and of the predominance of upward mobility.

Business Cycles and Social Mobility

The effect of business cycles on social mobility has been hitherto much more rarely discussed and analysed. The reason for this is mainly the fact that there are scarcely any adequate analyses of fluctuations in social mobility. The most important exception is the investigation by Pourcher, already referred to, which, because of its more circumspect conceptualisation, was in a far better position than other retrospective sociological analyses to ascertain when the interviewees were occupationally mobile and moved up or down. Pourcher is able to show that the rates of social mobility during the phase of prosperity at the beginning of the twentieth century rose, and that they stagnated or even fell at the latest from the Great Depression until the end of the Second World War and then rose again steeply during the following phase of prosperity until the time of the survey in 1959 (see Figure 2.1). The most obvious interpretation of his data is that the long economic swings strongly influenced the development of social mobility. During phases of long-term prosperity, the rates of social mobility rose steeply, while during phases of economic depression they stagnated or fell slightly. One could deduce from this a slight increase in social mobility rates over the long term, since, in spite of the business cycles, the modern economy has grown over the long run. In his latest study of the development of social mobility in the Federal Republic, Gerhard Kleining also regards the postwar phase of prosperity as an important reason for a strong increase in social mobility, but beyond this is unable to draw firm conclusions concerning the trend. A further indication of the connexion between business cycles and social mobility is provided by the difference between the results produced by the recent, fairly optimistic studies of social mobility, carried out after a long phase of prosperity, and the older studies which, after a period of economic disorder, came to more pessimistic conclusions. Studies which concern themselves with this relationship appear particularly desirable because many retrospective studies of social mobility have only appeared to deal with the trend of social mobility, but in actual fact have been dealing with little more than one of the long cycles of economic activity and the results inevitably varied depending on the date of the investigation.

Demographic Change

The impact of demographic factors on developments in the twentieth century has also scarcely been investigated. So far two theories have been formulated, although they have not yet been confirmed and documented by historical research. Boudon has produced a model to show how mobility rates were affected by changes in the social differentials of birthrates. He proceeded from the assumption – a rather improbable one for the twentieth century – that the birthrate of the lower strata rose in comparison with that of other strata. He came to the conclusion that changes in the birthrate of a particular class had no influence on the development of social mobility. As far as he was concerned, this was an argument in favour of the stagnation thesis. Duncan has investigated how, during the twentieth century, the relative increase in the birth rates of the upper middle class over the long term affected social mobility. He regarded this as a decisive reason for the stagnation of social mobility in American society during the twentieth century, but did not, however, rate this factor very highly. Since similar changes in the birth rates of particular strata are possible in other industrial countries in the twentieth century, it will be necessary to recognise that the demographic development represents an important, if not necessarily decisive, factor in the stagnation of social mobility.

'Policies for Equality of Opportunity'

The effects of political decisions and of changes in the political structure on social mobility in the twentieth century have so far only been discussed unsystematically. Significantly, there is no comprehensive term such as, for example, 'mobility policies' or 'policies for equality of opportunity'. There can be little doubt that political pressure in support of improved occupational opportunities and more equality of opportunity increased during the twentieth century as indeed can be gathered from numerous party and government programmes. But the question to what extent political decisions altered social mobility in the twentieth century remains an open one. Particular aspects such as the effect of educational policy, referred to above, encourage a sceptical assessment. Changes in the selection of applicants and in the criteria for promotion within the state administration, which can be documented for Germany, and which affect an increasingly important group of occupations, tend to support the theory of a slight increase in social mobility. Taken together, the political decisions, reforms and structural changes of the first two-thirds of the twentieth century have probably not caused any big increase in the rates of social mobility, but have helped to determine whether there was stagnation or a slight increase in social mobility.

Social Mentalities and Social Mobility

Those researching on mobility are broadly in agreement that there is no society in which the extent of social mobility can be explained in terms of changes in the occupational structure, educational opportunities, demographic changes, and political barriers and decisions alone. The question, therefore, of how changes in social mentality, values and motivations for moving up the social scale have influenced social mobility and its historical development is crucial but one that has scarcely been discussed. Whether or not the weak tendency among industrial workers in the nineteenth century to be mobile increased in the twentieth century and thus accelerated the rates of social mobility or whether it remained unchanged; whether or not the motivation of white-collar workers and civil servants to move up the social scale weakened as a result of their growing consciousness of their role as wage earners, with their increasing organisation in trade unions, and with the weakening of a distinct sense of middle-class status, and adapted itself to that of the industrial workers; whether or not the tendency of farmers and artisans to be immobile changed with the increasing capitalisation of the agrarian sector and of small-scale industry — all these are open questions.

Summing up the results of research on the trend of social mobility since the industrial revolution, one is struck by three main developments: firstly, it has become evident in recent years that the effects of the industrial revolution on social mobility have frequently been overestimated, and that, while industrialisation in Western Europe as well as in the USA did lead to enormous geographical mobility, it produced far less social mobility and remarkably little upward mobility. Secondly, recent analyses of industrial countries in the twentieth century show that the stagnation thesis cannot be sustained as a general rule. Above all, recent work on the USA and West European countries such as France, Britain and the Federal Republic of Germany confirm a slight increase in social mobility rates which has not, however, removed the high degree of inequality of opportunity. If one looks for explanations for the development of social mobility, demographic factors and the expansion of education seem to have reinforced or at least not prevented the stagnation of social mobility and also to have produced changes in the social structure in the direction of a slight increase in social mobility. Historical research on social mobility will, however, have to concentrate on dealing with political decisions and changes in social mentality before it can both document the conflicting theories on the stagnation or the slight increase in social mobility, and also provide plausible explanations. Thirdly, the majority of studies on the trend of social mobility in the twentieth century remain unsatisfactory — perhaps even more so than this research report has shown — because they do not take social history seriously enough and are scarcely interested in the historical causes and conditions of social mobility. Most account is taken of changes in the occupational and social structures because they can easily be read off mobility tables. Other factors of social mobility such as changes in social attitudes, the effects of wars, business cycles, political decisions and processes are normally disregarded. Partial answers to these questions can be found in a different category of studies which nearly always deal with individual aspects of social mobility: analyses of possibilities for upward mobility among industrial workers, of equality of opportunity in the educational sector, and finally, studies of the recruitment of elites. The following chapters will deal with these questions.

3 OPPORTUNITIES FOR UPWARD MOBILITY AMONG INDUSTRIAL WORKERS

The question of the development of opportunities for occupational and upward mobility among industrial workers has been a topic for discussion ever since the beginnings of industrialisation in Europe and the USA. It was already being dealt with by nineteenth-century social scientists such as de Tocqueville, Engels and Sombart.[1] Three main problems stimulated empirical historical research which did not, however, get seriously under way until after the Second World War for the reasons given above. The starting point of the research was the striking contrast between the history of modern class conflict and socialist movements in the USA as compared with Europe. The more highly developed class consciousness of European workers has repeatedly been explained in terms of the more limited prospects of improving their material position through individual effort and of moving up the social scale. It has been the aim of a considerable number of investigations to reappraise this argument. They deal almost exclusively with the nineteenth century, during which both opportunities for mobility and class consciousness in Europe appear to have differed very sharply from the situation prevailing in the USA. Secondly, the discussion of the development of the standard of living of industrial workers and of the advantages and disadvantages of modernisation for the material position of various social strata also dealt with the distribution of opportunities for occupational and upward mobility. Although there is no consensus on how the importance of inequality of opportunity should be evaluated as compared with other aspects of their material position — such as the exercise of authority by plant management, job security, real wages, housing, medical provision — nevertheless, equality of opportunity is one of the standard, if not always central, topics of these debates about living standards and social inequality. Historical research has above all been concerned with the question of the social consequences of the industrial revolution in Europe and the USA. Thirdly, research on the development of working-class culture has strengthened interest in the question of the perception of inequality of opportunity and of upward mobility. Studies of this kind concentrate primarily on investigating whether the emergence of a working-class culture in the nineteenth century is reflected in a particular concept of equality of opportunity and of upward social mobility among workers which does not coincide with bourgeois ideas of social success. A number of historical studies of the late eighteenth and nineteenth centuries were written, particularly after the Second World War, covering all these aspects, whereas there are hardly any investigations of the historical developments in the twentieth century. In most of these works the three questions referred to, which provide the framework for the analysis of the opportunities for occupational and upward mobility among workers (the political consequences of social mobility, standards of living, and working-class culture), are merged together. Moreover, in most countries research on the development of opportunities for occupational and upward mobility among the industrial working class is controversial. Even where research does not lead directly to controversy, it tends to produce conflicting and random results unrelated to each other. There is frequently a pessimistic school, which regards the industrial revolution as an unfavourable period with even an increase in inequality of opportunity among workers, and an optimistic school which considers that the opportunities for occupational and upward mobility among industrial workers during industrialisation at the very least improved and may even be considered to have been favourable.

The opportunities for occupational and upward mobility among industrial workers in the USA during the industrial revolution have been investigated in a series of case studies, which are based on similar sources — such as census lists, city directories, marriage-licence files — which are invariably studies of towns, and which normally use similar methods. The results by no means all coincide (see Tables 3.1 and 3.2). The results of the first case study by Stephan Thernstrom (already referred to) contradicted the myth of the USA as 'the land of opportunities'. Thernstrom shows that in Newburyport, a textile town in New England with a high proportion of Irish immigrants, between 1850 and 1880 only 15 per cent of unskilled workers moved up into skilled and non-manual jobs (in the course of a decade). The sons of these unskilled workers were certainly more successful within the working class; the non-manual occupations, however, remained closed to them as well. Thernstrom sees the main reason for these disappointingly low rates of upward mobility in the fact that the unskilled workers of Newburyport preferred to feel secure socially rather than to move up occupationally. They tried to become house owners by exploiting the whole of the family's labour force and income, investing their savings and sacrificing their own further education and an improved education for their children to this end. Half of the unskilled workers of Newburyport

Table 3.1: The rise of workers' sons into non-manual occupations in North American and European cities 1830-1950 (percentage outflow)

	Newburyport USA (1)	Poughkeepsie USA (2)	Boston USA (3)	Indianapolis USA (4)	Hamilton Canada (5)	Marseilles France (6)	Copenhagen Denmark (7)	Västeras Sweden (8)	Cologne Germany (9)	Euskirchen Germany (10)	Bochum Germany (11)	Esslingen Germany (12)
1830												
1840									18	8		
1850	0				7	14	21					48
1860	7											
1870	9								15	18		45
1880	10	26										
1890			41					26				
1900											12	
1910			41	22					18	17		39

Sources: Col. 1: S. Thernstrom, *Poverty and Progress. Social Mobility in a Nineteenth Century City* (Cambridge, 1964), p. 110; col. 2: C. Griffen, 'Making it in America', *New York History*, 51 (1970) p. 485; col. 3: S. Thernstrom, *The Other Bostonians* (Cambridge, 1973), p. 244; col. 4: N. Rogoff, *Recent Trends in Occupational Mobility* (Glencoe, 1953); col. 5: M.B. Katz, *The People of Hamilton, Canada West* (Cambridge, Mass., 1975), p. 172; col. 6: W.H. Sewell, 'Social Mobility in a 19th century European City', *Journal of Interdisciplinary History*, 7 (1976), p. 221; col. 7: T. Rishoy, 'Metropolitan Social Mobility 1850-1950', *Quality and Quantity*, 5 (1971), p. 136f; col. 8: S. Akerman, *Migration and Social Mobility: Some Findings from the Three-city Study*, mimeograph (Uppsala, 1974), p. 8; col. 9: H. Daheim, 'Berufliche Intergenerationen-Mobilität in der komplexen Gesellschaft', *Kölner Zeitschrift für Soziologie*, 16 (1964), p. 117ff (1833-40, 1870-77, 1906-13); col. 10: R. Mayntz, *Euskirchen*, p. 154ff (1833-40, 1870-77, 1906-13); col. 11: D. Crew, 'Definitions of Modernity: Social Mobility in a German Town, 1880-1901', *Journal of Social History*, 7 (fall, 1973), p. 61; col. 12: H. Schomerus, 'Ausbildung und Aufstiegsmöglichkeiten württembergischer Metallarbeiter 1850 bis 1914 am Beispiel der Maschinenfabrik Esslingen' in U. Engelhardt, V. Sellin & E. Stuke (eds.) *Soziale Bewegung und politische Verfassung* (Stuttgart, 1977), p. 390 and information provided by the author from hitherto unpublished data (1846-70, 1870-1914).

Table 3.2: The rise of workers into non-manual occupations in North American and European cities 1830-1950 (per cent)

	Boston USA	Pough-keepsie USA	Waltham USA	Atlanta USA	Omaha USA	Birming-ham USA	Los Angeles USA	Norris-town USA	Hamilton Canada	Bochum Germany	Preston England	Rotter-dam Nether-lands	Oskars-ham Sweden
	(1)	(2)	(3)	(4)	(5)	(6)	(7)	(8)	(9)	(10)	(11)	(12)	(13)
1830-40	9											5	
1840-50	10	17	10										
1850-60	18	18	15						16		5	7	
1860-70		13	13										
1870-80				11									
1880-90	12				21	24							
1890-00						16				8			
1900-10					23	32							10
1910-20	22						16	9					
1920-30								10					
1930-40	11							10					
1940-50													

Sources: cols. 1-2, 5, 7-8: Thernstrom, *Other Bostonians*, p. 234; col. 3: H.M. Gitelman, *Workingmen of Waltham. Mobility in American Urban Industrial Development 1850-1890* (Baltimore, London, 1974), p. 66; col. 4: R.J. Hopkins, 'Occupational and Geographic Mobility in Atlanta, 1870-1896', *Journal of Southern History*, 34 (1968), p. 205; col. 6: P.B. Worthman, 'Working-class Mobility in Birmingham, Alabama, 1880-1914', in T.K. Hareven (ed.), *Anonymous Americans* (Englewood Cliffs, 1971), p. 198; col. 9: Katz, *The People of Hamilton*, p. 144; col. 10: Crew, 'Definitions of Modernity', p. 53; col. 11: M. Anderson, *Family Structure in 19th Century Lancashire* (Cambridge, 1971), p. 28; col. 12: H. van Dijk, 'De beroepsmobiliteit in Rotterdam in de negentiende eeuw' in J. van Herwaarden (ed.), *Lof der historie* (Rotterdam, 1974), p. 143ff; col. 13: B. Ohngren & D. Papp, *Arbetarna vid Oskarsham varv kring sekelskiftet*, p. 30.

and the majority of the Irish immigrants among them did in fact become house owners in the course of their occupational careers. Thernstrom believes that the myth of the 'land of opportunities' remained unbroken despite minimal opportunities for occupational upward mobility because for many unskilled workers there was the real chance of becoming house owners and, therefore, respected members of the community.

Prompted by this study, several other analyses of workers, or of the entire populations of towns of this period, were carried out which, however, only partially confirmed Thernstrom's pessimistic assessment. Closest to Thernstrom's main thesis were the results of the studies by Stuart Blumin, already referred to, who analysed social mobility in Philadelphia before the actual industrial revolution, i.e. during the phase of expanding commercial capitalism and high Irish immigration rates, and who found low upward mobility rates and high downward mobility rates between 1820 and 1860. In his methodologically sophisticated work on Boston between 1830 and 1860, Peter Knight also seems to have come to a rather pessimistic assessment of upward social mobility (see Tables 3.1 and 3.2).

Studies of some other American towns in the latter part of the nineteenth century, on the other hand, reveal different results. Clyde Griffen analysed social mobility between 1850 and 1880 in Poughkeepsie, a slowly expanding small commercial town in New York State, with high levels of Irish and German immigration, and was particularly interested in the differences in opportunities for occupational and upward mobility between groups of ethnic immigrants and the native-born population. According to his results, the opportunities for occupational and upward mobility among black or Irish immigrant workers were unfavourable. Only a small proportion of them moved up into better paid jobs and occupations requiring qualifications, while the native-born workers, on the other hand, had quite favourable chances for occupational and upward mobility. Up to one third moved up into non-manual jobs. They became owners of small craft and retail shops with particular frequency. Griffen shows that these differences in mobility were not dependent on the different religious denominations of Irish and German immigrants and the occupational values connected with them, but above all on the far superior occupational qualifications of immigrants from Germany. This could also be the decisive reason for the differences between this example and Thernstrom's test case of Newburyport. But Griffen also stresses that the social elevation of the German immigrants was restricted to the small-scale clothing and foodstuffs trades which were economically less secure and often paid less than skilled working-class occupations. Alan Dawley investigated the opportunities for upward movement among shoe workers in Lynn (Massachusetts) between 1870 and 1880. It is also his view that the borderline between manual and non-manual occupations was not an unsurmountable barrier since between every fifth and sixth shoeworker was able to get into a non-manual occupation within a decade. He too stresses, of course, that there are no spectacular career opportunities, but usually an upward movement from skilled working-class occupations into the lower ranks of the non-manual occupations. Two other investigations of the southern states of the USA limit still further the general validity of Thernstrom's results. Paul B. Worthman, who investigated Birmingham (Alabama) between 1880 and 1914, a town which rapidly expanded after the Civil War, assessed the opportunities for upward movement among the industrial workers favourably. After 25 years of employment, almost half the workers of Birmingham had moved up into non-manual occupations. Their rates of occupational upward mobility were thus considerably higher than those of the workers in Newburyport. In his analysis of Atlanta, after the Civil War one of the most important cities in the South, which also prospered during the period 1870 to 1890, Richard Hopkins reached similar conclusions. Hopkins did stress the extraordinarily unfavourable opportunities for upward movement among the black workers, which lead him to a sceptical assessment of Reconstruction . But he found hardly any difference in the opportunities for mobility between white immigrants and the white indigenous population. Twenty-two per cent (native-born population) and 21 per cent (immigrants) of the white workers of Atlanta moved up into non-manual occupations within a decade and thus also had superior opportunities compared with the workers of Newburyport, Boston or Philadelphia. However, the question of the reasons for these unusually high rates of mobility among white workers in Atlanta remains an open one. Industrialisation and migration do not appear to have played a central role since, although Atlanta grew rapidly, the share of industry in the city's economy and the percentage of immigrants in its population both remained small. A study of the Midwest has also failed to confirm Thernstrom's theory. In his book on the heavy engineering town of South Bend, Dean R. Esslinger reached the optimistic conclusion that the opportunities for upward movement between 1850 and 1880 were much more favourable than in Newburyport, i.e. for occupational, property holding and intergenerational mobility. Esslinger explains this partly in terms of the peculiarities of the Midwest: the proportion of skilled immigrants who were not without means was higher in South Bend than on the East Coast, since the immigration into the interior of the United States filtered out a percentage of the poor and unqualified immigrants. Moreover, the rapid industrialisation and urbanisation of South Bend opened up favourable opportunities for moving up at least into skilled and semi-skilled working-class occupations. Finally, Howard P. Chudacoff's study of Omaha (Nebraska), so far the only real frontier town which has been investigated, with an explosive growth rate following high levels of Irish and German immigration, reveals high rates of upward and downward mobility. Within the span of a decade, every fifth worker had moved up into a non-manual occupation.[2]

These American studies had a 'pioneer function' for research on the social history of European countries since they have developed methods of quantification which, suitably modified, can be applied to Europe as well, since they have made the question of social mobility and equality of opportunity a standard topic of social history, and since they have abandoned the traditional one-sided emphasis on the analysis of elite recruitment and have placed the opportunities for occupational and upward mobility of the Common Man — and above all of industrial workers — at the centre of their work. Moreover, an appropriate form for the historical analysis of social mobility, namely the urban study, has been repeatedly applied and thereby improved, and has also been used — particularly by Thernstrom — for historical comparisons within the modest framework of existing possibilities.[3] In the meantime, however, disadvantages of these urban studies which limit the extent to which they can be applied to European history have become apparent. In the first place, in order to cut down the work involved usually no more than three decades are covered. The effects of the industrial revolution are not discernable in this relatively short timespan, since one cannot draw comparisons with the stages of pre-industrial and advanced industrial development. Secondly, while through urban studies it was possible to investigate certain important factors affecting mobility such as savings, house ownership, the situations of ethnic groups, and recently also the family, as far as other equally crucial factors affecting mobility are concerned such as avenues to and barriers against upward movement in business or in education, studies of firms or historical studies of education systems have proved more fruitful. The effects of changes in the occupational structure and in the mentality towards mobility on the social elevation of industrial workers have usually been ignored; only Thernstrom and Griffen have touched on these questions. Moreover, despite the tradition of American community power research, the American studies have almost invariably remained peculiarly blind to political factors affecting social mobility — also at local government level. Finally, a model of historical stratification has become established in American mobility studies which is only concerned with mobility among 'low manual workers', 'skilled manual workers', 'lower white-collar' and 'higher white-collar workers'. This stratification model has hardly ever been tested against historical reality. Its main weakness lies in the fact that within the category of 'white-collar' it does not distinguish between employees and the self-employed. The conditions determining the elevation of industrial workers into these two social spheres were fundamentally different. Morever, the shifts between these two groups in the late nineteenth and twentieth centuries represent crucial developments in social mobility which cannot be perceived on the basis of the stratification model used in American mobility studies.[4] Despite such reservations, this American line of research can have important and positive repercussions for the investigation of the opportunities for upward social mobility among workers in Europe. There are particular indications of this in the research on French and German workers which we shall have to return to.

The opportunities for occupational and upward mobility among workers during the industrialisation of England and Scotland have not been investigated in uniform local studies using quantification methods, to the same extent as in the USA. Instead, they have been dealt with incidentally in scattered studies on very varied topics. It is, therefore, much more difficult to summarise these assessments in a research survey. Nevertheless, one can mention two focal points of research: the textile workers of the late eighteenth and nineteenth centuries and the labour aristocracy from the middle of the nineteenth century onwards.

The analyses of English textile workers have reached the more or less unanimous conclusion that the opportunities for upward movement at the time of the actual industrial revolution, and also in the course of the remaining years of the nineteenth century, were extraordinarily unfavourable and that only a few industrial workers or their sons moved up into non-manual occupations which offered a higher income, a secure social position, or prestige. According to Duncan Bythell, who investigated the decline of handloom weaving in the early nineteenth century, the occupational opportunities of this group, which was particularly hard hit by the industrial revolution, were largely restricted to the other working-class occupations within the textile industry. Bythell does see certain possibilities for upward movement into skilled working-class occupations but does not mention any cases of elevation into non-manual occupations. Michael Sanderson tried to prove that in Lancashire between the late eighteenth and early nineteenth centuries, during the emergence of the textile industry, the opportunities for education and upward movement among workers and workers' children were not simply unfavourable but actually deteriorated. Sanderson argued that before the beginning of the industrial revolution the charity schools were an important 'channel for the elevation' of working-class children into better-paid, non-manual occupations requiring qualifications, and demonstrated through the example of a particular charity school in this region that none of the workers' sons among the pupils of this school himself became a worker. In Sanderson's view, this 'channel of elevation' closed with the emergence of the cotton industry, since the school attendance of workers' children declined because of child labour and the lack of schools in the new textile centres. With the help of marriage documents of the 1830s Sanderson demonstrates much lower rates of upward mobility for workers' children and a high rate of downward mobility. Sanderson's argument has been rightly criticised since he compared school documents which only record the upwardly mobile working-class children with marriage documents which rather understate upward mobility. All the same, his essay is a stimulating contribution to the study of the development of opportunities for education and for occupational and upward mobility during the industrial revolution. In his model study of family structure in the nineteenth century, Michael Anderson also deals with Lancashire. He too had quantitive data only for the limited period 1840-60 at his disposal and here too only for a particular district of the town of Preston with which his work primarily deals. Although Anderson gained the impression that occupational mobility was remarkably high, only a very small number of workers actually moved up into skilled or semi-skilled occupations. Within a decade only 6 per cent of the textile workers and, outside the textile industry, only 4 per cent of the skilled workers and not a single unskilled worker had become self-employed. Anderson's main thesis is that during the industrial revolution — despite migration and separation from the home and workplace — the family was still of great importance for individual social status; it did not, however, facilitate social elevation so much as the preservation of the existing standard of living, which was invariably threatened by unemployment, illness, death and large families.

The question of the opportunities for upward mobility among the English and Scottish labour aristocracy, which have mainly been investigated for the period from the middle of the nineteenth century onwards, is, however, a contentious issue. In his pioneering article on the labour aristocracy in England during the Victorian era, Eric J. Hobsbawm regarded the opportunities for upward mobility among this stratum of workers as favourable and saw in this one reason among others for their adopting middle-class values, and for their non-radical political attitude. Hobsbawm's theory is supported by the results of J.F.C. Harrison's study of the self-help organisations of English workers in the education field. According to Harrison, the 'mechanics' institutes', which were mainly supported by the labour aristocracy and which emerged in the 1830s with a membership by 1861 of 300,000, offered favourable opportunities for moving up from the working class into white-collar and entrepreneurial positions. Harrison quotes the example of one school whose pupils in 1842 came mainly from working-class families and of whom twenty years later most had become white-collar employees; a third of them were even successful businessmen. In Trygve Tholfsen's view, the Victorian elementary schools aimed to stimulate the motivation for upward mobility not only among the labour aristocracy but also among other working-class groups, and thereby to indoctrinate them with an essential element of the Victorian middle-class ethos. To what extent this goal was achieved, how far traditional working-class radicalism resisted this ethos and how many workers' children did in fact rise socially via this school system — these are all questions which Tholfsen leaves open.

Geoffrey Crossick, who investigated the concepts of and opportunities for upward movement among the labour aristocracy in three London suburbs in the middle of the nineteenth century, contradicts this view. He reckons that even members of the labour aristocracy could rarely advance higher than the level of small master craftsmen and considers that in terms of their mentality and economic position these craftsmen belong to the working class rather than the middle class. Above all, he shows that the career ambitions of members of the labour aristocracy were not geared towards moving up into the middle class but rather towards achieving a respected and independent position within the working class. In Crossick's view individualistic motivations towards upward mobility were foreign to the mentality of the members of the labour aristocracy. In his analysis of the labour aristocracy in Edinburgh between 1850 and 1900 Robert Q. Gray comes to similar conclusions as Crossick. Social values of the Edinburgh labour aristocracy such as respectability, independence and social elevation, did derive — according to Gray — from the middle class but were reinterpreted in the context of the living conditions of the workers and did not aim for individual social ascent but rather for the preservation of the standard of living of the individual family, which was continually under threat, and for independence from public charity and the workhouse. Gray, moreover, gained the impression that in Edinburgh the occupational mobility of members of the labour aristocracy very rarely actually led to middle-class occupations but at most to jobs like a subordinate white-collar worker, a master craftsman or a primary school teacher, which lay on the borderline between the middle and working classes.[5]

On the whole, British research on the opportunities for occupational and upward mobility among industrial workers during the eighteenth and nineteenth centuries is still in its initial stages. Further development will depend to a large extent on whether access to quantifiable sources, which is at present extremely difficult, improves. Conditions for historical research on mobility are, however, unusually favourable in Great Britain, since British social historians have for some time devoted research efforts to a number of important factors which help determine the social mobility of workers — such as family structure, education and working-class culture. As a result, these factors could be given greater consideration in studies of historical mobility than has been the case in other countries.

The social mobility of French workers during industrialisation has also scarcely been investigated and then mainly in very recent studies. On the basis of his analysis of the workers in the textile city of Lille, Pierre Pierrard makes a very pessimistic assessment similar to the conclusions reached by the English research on the Lancashire textile industry and Thernstrom's study of Newburyport. The mass of the unskilled workers had in effect no opportunity to acquire training in skills. Pierrard stresses above all the sharp contrast between the opportunities for upward mobility among the workers' elite compared with the mass of the workers. Only the better paid working-class elite received an extended period of education, attend the *école primaire supérieure*, which provided access to further education or to white-collar positions, or (in the 1850s and 1860s) to adult evening classes. Admittedly, Pierrard deals almost exclusively with educational opportunities. He does not deal either qualitatively or quantitively with the social origins of, or with the opportunities for, occupational or upward movement among the workers of Lille. In an article on the workers of

Marseilles, which is strongly influenced by American research pre-occupations and methods, William H. Sewell Jr makes a similar pessimistic assessment. Although Marseilles expanded rapidly after 1820 and enjoyed an economic boom, only 13 per cent of workers' sons in Marseilles moved up into non-manual occupations around 1850. What is particularly interesting is the explanation which Sewell gives for this development. He considers that these low rates of upward mobility are not caused by socioeconomic barriers but rather by the values held by these Marseilles workers: as a result of their class consciousness, they preferred to remain in the working class and to leave numerous opportunities for upward movement untapped. Sewell proved this point above all with the fact that the farmers' sons in Marseilles, who did not share these values and were therefore more inclined to seize occupational opportunities, moved up into non-manual occupations more frequently (18 per cent). From this Sewell draws the general conclusion that European workers in the nineteenth century had fewer opportunities for moving up the social scale than American workers because their class consciousness, formed by guild traditions, concealed from them opportunities for upward movement or made such opportunities appear unattractive. His article certainly ranks among the most stimulating pieces of work in the field of historical research on social mobility. Two questions, however, still remain open: first, even the rates of upward mobility of farmers' sons in Marseilles are far below the rates of upward mobility in the city of Boston, which Sewell − rightly or wrongly − uses above all for the purposes of comparison (see Table 3.3). Thus, the differences between the USA and Europe were not wholly dependent on the values of the workers. Secondly, he pays too little attention to the question of what the values of the workers were based on. Above all, he does not mention to what extent the society of Marseilles as a whole differed from the society of, for example, Boston or Philadelphia, and how far the values of the workers represented reactions to the behaviour of the middle class. All the same, Sewell's theory of the low upward mobility rates of workers − in the context of the French lower class − is also supported by Theresa McBride's study of English and French domestic servants in the nineteenth century. McBride, who uses mainly French material for the question of upward social mobility, demonstrates surprisingly high rates of upward mobility for female servants. With the aid of savings and by gaining housekeeping experience, which the transitional occupation of servant could provide, roughly a third of female servants achieved through marriage a social status which was above that of their parents.

In contrast to Sewell, in her study of the miners of Carmaux, Rolande Trempé investigated how the recruitment of workers affected class consciousness. Whereas in the middle of the century most of the miners still came from families of small peasants and farm labourers in the vicinity of Carmaux, later on, to an increasing extent, they came from urban miners' families. At the same time, the miners changed from being farmers who worked underground only as a sideline, or even only occasionally (*paysan mineur*), into modern industrial workers, who were economically dependent exclusively on their wages (*ouvrier mineur*). Trempé regards these changes as key factors in the growing willingness of the miners of Carmaux to strike and to organise after the middle of the century. In contrast to Sewell, however, Trempé leaves open the question of the extent and the consequences of opportunities for occupational and upward mobility. She only mentions that supervisory posts were almost exclusively filled with workers from the society of the pit; she does not deal with the origins of the 'miners elite' — the machinists working above ground.

In her study of the glass workers of Carmaux, Joan Scott sees social mobility from the same perspective as Rolande Trempée. Scott concentrates on the social effects of the gradual mechanisation of the glass-blowing industry which changed glass workers from a socially isolated, highly paid labour elite, who inside France were very mobile within their own occupation with high rates of self-recruitment, into a semi-skilled, still fairly highly paid working-class group from the vicinity of Carmaux, recruited from very varied sections of the middle and lower social strata. Scott regards qualifications, size of income and social origins as important reasons for the fact that glass workers — in contrast to the miners of Carmaux — rarely went on strike and — apart from the traditional glassblowers' elite, whose qualifications had become obsolescent — only infrequently organised themselves in unions.

Other studies which, like those of Trempé and Scott, deal with the social origins rather than the occupational opportunities of workers, put more stress on the low social mobility of French workers. In his study of the workers of the industrial region of Lyon, Yves Lequin comes to the conclusion that even in the 1850s one cannot speak of high mobility and *déracination* at all. The workers came mainly from the region itself; immigrants had no problems adapting themselves either, since most of them came from working-class families or even had the same manual occupations as their fathers. In an article on the linen-printing plant of Oberkampf, situated in a purely agricultural area, Serge Chassagne, A. Dewerpe and Y. Gaulupeau show that, soon

after the establishment of the factory, the skilled workers, in particular, were to a large extent recruited from local working-class families.
In an article on the French foundry workers, Denis Woronoff showed
that the skilled and respected labour aristocracy, which was privileged
with wide supervisory functions and in close contact with the management, was frequently recruited from a few local families from this
stratum of workers. In an investigation of the workers in the French
iron industry between 1800 and 1870, Gerd Hardach confirms the
stability of the labour aristocracy and, moreover, points out that the
unskilled workers in this branch of industry developed from being
seasonal migrant workers into more steady full-time workers, who came
to a large extent from agriculture and were shaped by agrarian attitudes
and values.[6]

On the whole, research on French workers during the period of industrialisation has dealt mainly with their social origins and rarely with
their opportunities for occupational and upward mobility. As a result,
it has ignored one of the factors which was important for the development of the social consciousness of workers. There can be no doubt,
however, that among the works referred to above are some of the best
conceived, most thoroughly researched, fruitful and stimulating studies
of the emergence of a working class in Europe. The depth and quality
of their previous research is such as to suggest that if French scholars
were to take up the question of opportunities for occupational and
upward mobility among workers they would produce important results.

Studies of the opportunities for upward movement among German
workers during the industrial revolution have nearly all been published
recently. Among them there are relatively few works by West German
historians. The pessimistic view predominates here too. In an investigation of the Berlin working class before the revolution of 1848, the
American historian, Frederick Marquardt, came to the conclusion
that the opportunities for social ascent were unfavourable for both
unskilled and skilled workers and were probably even less favourable
than those of eighteenth century artisans. By this he means primarily
social ascent to the level of an independent artisan, but also into
posts as supervisory white-collar employees of early industrial firms.
Marquardt sees the most important barriers to upward movement as
lack of capital and education. The costs of setting up a craft shop, of
attending secondary school or of a trade apprenticeship in a prosperous
trade were considerably higher than the income or the conceivable
savings of the Berlin workers. In view of the mentality of the Berlin

workers, the prospect of moving up into better paid, non-manual or economically independent occupations did not appear particularly attractive. Only the Berlin labour aristocracy had more favourable initial opportunities since they had better occupational training, higher and steadier incomes and shared occupational values which were geared more towards social advancement. Marquardt does not consider the political consequences of these barriers to upward movement to be particularly significant. While he puts forward the theory that class consciousness developed among the Berlin workers as early as the 1840s, he does not see this as a consequence of the restrictions on upward mobility so much as the result of the development of their standard of living, the rapid growth in population, and socioeconomic and political discrimination on the part of the middle class. Lacking reliable sources, however, Marquardt was unable to document his theories on social mobility quantitatively, but only on the basis of individual cases. Neither could he make clear how typical the details of the Berlin case were of other German industrial regions. The merits of his article are first, the fact that, on the basis of his own investigations of the social structure of the Berlin working class before 1848, he can assess upward and downward movement much more accurately than the usual mobility studies: and secondly, the fact that he is particularly concerned to determine the causes of and restrictions on social mobility and, in addition to economic barriers, also incorporates social mentality and political structure in his analysis. Peter Lundgreen deals with a particular aspect of the opportunities for upward mobility among workers, namely access to technical training during the industrial revolution, in another study to which we shall have to return later. His results too permit the conclusion that the opportunities for training, and therefore for social advance among the lower strata, deteriorated around the middle of the century.

The East German historian Hartmut Zwahr's work on the social structure of the Leipzig workers covers a slightly later period. In an article which contains selective results from a larger study, Zwahr endeavoured to prove that the proportion of 'born proletarians', i.e. workers from working-class families among the book printers, compositors and manual workers in Leipzig, increased between about 1830 and 1870. Since in his view born proletarians are more class conscious than workers from other social groups, he sees in this a decisive factor for the emergence of an organised workers' movement in Leipzig. The importance of Zwahr's investigation lies in the fact that it introduced into research on historical mobility a new category of sources — the so-called '*Schutzprotokolle*', that it was the first historical work in East Germany to deal empirically with the social mobility of industrial workers and that it examines a branch of industry in which class consciousness and workers' organisations developed particularly early. His main thesis, however, has so far not yet been fully documented: the born proletarians showed a long-term increase only among the book printers; in the other two categories of workers investigated by Zwahr while fluctuations can be observed in the periods for which the sample is sufficient, no such long-term trend is apparent. Moreover, Zwahr has only investigated the social origins of the industrial workers and not the opportunities for upward mobility, which is, in fact, the aspect of mobility which a long tradition of social research − to which Engels made an important contribution − has always associated with class consciousness. Finally, it remains unclear how far investigations of the commercial city of Leipzig can help to elucidate the effects of the industrial revolution on social mobility. One would really have preferred Zwahr to have investigated an industrial city in Saxony.

Finally, for the late nineteenth century, the American historian, David Crew, has investigated the case of an industrial city − Bochum in the Ruhr. In Crew's opinion, the opportunities of the Bochum workers for upward movement were poor − less favourable than the opportunities of American industrial workers for, during the period 1880-90, only 6 per cent of unskilled workers and 10 per cent of skilled workers moved up into non-manual occupations and only 12 per cent even of workers' sons secured occupations outside the working class. Like Marquardt, Crew demonstrates the extraordinarily wide differences in opportunities for upward movement within the working class. While unskilled workers had extremely poor opportunities for mobility, every fourth skilled worker and nearly every fifth son of a skilled worker moved up into non-manual jobs. (See Tables 3.3. and 3.4). Crew explains the low overall upward mobility not only in terms of the barriers imposed by lack of education and of capital, but also in terms of the social mentality of the Bochum workers. Security and home ownership seemed more important to them than an expensive education for their children, the collective improvement or the maintenance of the status of their own occupational group more important than opportunities for individual advancement. In Crew's view, the decisive reason for these preferences was the traditional emphasis on occupational status of the Bochum workers. Crew's work is important because it applies for the first time the quantitative methods of historical research on mobility developed in the USA to a German case

Table 3.3: The occupational career mobility of Bochum workers 1880-1901 (per cent)

Occupation in 1880	Occupation in 1890/1901											
	In same occupation		Other unskilled/ semi-skilled work		Other skilled work		Unskilled and semi-skilled work		Skilled/artisanal work		Non-manual work	
	1890 (1)	1901 (2)	1890 (3)	1901 (4)	1890 (5)	1901 (6)	1890 (7)	1901 (8)	1890 (9)	1901 (10)	1890 (11)	1901 (12)
Day labourers	33.3	8.7	54.8	65.2					2.4	4.3	4.8	4.3
Unskilled factory workers	72.5	66.1	8.9	3.4					11.8	11.9	4.9	6.8
Miners	69.4	33.0	10.2	16.7					0.0	0.0	6.1	13.0
Skilled metal workers	71.4	58.8			0.0	0.0	9.5	17.6			14.3	17.7
Skilled workers building & construction	72.7	50.0			3.0	3.8	12.2	19.2			12.0	19.2
Skilled/artisanal: food, drink & clothing	79.5	70.4			2.9	0.0	7.8	0.0			7.8	14.8
Skilled/artisanal: wood, leather & luxury	80.6	52.9			0.0	0.0	6.4	5.9			9.7	29.4

Source: Based on Crew, 'Definitions of Modernity', tables 3 and 4.

Table 3.4: The intergenerational mobility of Bochum workers in 1900 (per cent)

Father's occupation	Son's occupation					
	Same as father	Same skill level	Total stable (1 & 2)	Higher skill level	Lower skill level	Non-manual
	(1)	(2)	(3)	(4)	(5)	(6)
Miners	44.0	10.2	54.2	27.1		19.0
Unskilled factory workers	40.0	25.8	65.8	28.1		5.9
Skilled metal workers	46.6	20.0	66.6		23.3	10.0
Skilled workers: building & construction	27.4	15.7	43.1		39.2	17.6
Skilled/artisanal: food, drink & clothing	23.0	33.3	56.3		31.3	12.3
Skilled/artisanal: wood, leather & luxury	16.7	37.4	54.1		29.1	16.6

Source: Based on Crew, 'Definitions of Modernity', table 6.

study and does so with discrimination and with considerable imaginative insight (in this respect it is far superior to the majority of investigations on American topics). In contrast to Thernstrom's investigation of Boston, however, Crew did not — presumably for financial reasons — follow the long-term development and was obliged, therefore, to leave open the question of how economic concentration and bureaucratisation, the decline of the petite bourgeoisie, the increase in the numbers of white-collar employees and the increasing formalisation of career training affected the opportunities of Bochum workers to move up the social scale. Furthermore, a comparison of the rates of mobility in Bochum and in American cities demonstrates that the differences were often insignificant and were conceivably overemphasised by Crew. If, at the end of the nineteenth century, 8 per cent of the workers in Bochum had moved up into non-manual occupations within a decade, 11 per cent in Atlanta, 12 per cent in Boston and 13 per cent in Poughkeepsie and Waltham, then the most striking feature is the similarity in the low rates of mobility (see Table 3.2).

A pessimistic assessment of the opportunities for social elevation among urban workers is also provided by an investigation by Lutz Niethammer of the housing situation of workers in Imperial Germany. While only peripherally concerned with vertical mobility, it indicates important conditions for inequality of opportunity. His pioneering empirical article shows that the housing situation was an important obstacle to social advancement: the mass of unskilled and/or newly arrived industrial workers got into a vicious circle of a tight housing market, high rents (and therefore high indebtedness), high and involuntary fluctuation in employment and housing, small and poorly equipped apartments, the impossibility of long-term career planning and, as a result of all these factors, poor opportunities for training and upward movement. Only a minority of skilled workers with a rising income and a higher degree of security of employment were able to exploit more effectively the limited opportunities for education and for social advance. Like the work of Thernstrom, Niethammer's article shows that high geographic mobility, at any rate before 1914, suggests a flight from unfavourable working and living conditions rather than a rational exploitation of the labour and accommodation markets and of the opportunities for education and upward mobility. Finally, support for the pessimistic assessment of the opportunities for social elevation open to German workers during industrialisation comes from general investigations of intergenerational mobility in Euskirchen and Cologne. In Euskirchen the proportion of workers' sons who became self-employed (without more precise differentiation) between the 1830s and the 1920s remained at approximately 2 per cent and in Cologne during the same period at 3-5 per cent.[7]

This pessimistic assessment is qualified by two studies of white-collar employees, although they only deal with workers' chances of upward movement as a side issue. In a case study of white-collar employees in the firm of Siemens before 1914, Jürgen Kocka established that skilled workers were frequently able to advance to foremen and, in the early phase of the firm — before about 1880 — even to works' manager. Factory experience was a vital qualification, especially in the early phase, because of the lack of formal training for employees. Kocka estimates that at this time at least half of the white-collar employees in Siemens were former workers. In her study of heavy industry in the Ruhr district during the last decades before the First World War, Elaine Glovka-Spencer reaches similar conclusions. The foremen in the iron and steel industry were very often skilled workers from this branch of industry who had been promoted; the majority of mine inspectors in the Ruhr mining industry also came from miners' families, although they were increasingly trained in mining colleges. Both investigations rightly focus their analysis on the recruitment of white-collar employees. As far as the opportunities of social ascent for workers are concerned, there were too few foremen's positions in heavy industry and the other white-collar occupations were too closed to workers for there to be high rates of upward mobility for workers. This combination of few opportunities for upward mobility among workers within the plant and open recruitment of low-ranking white-collar positions becomes particularly evident in Klaus Tenfelde's work on the Ruhr miners before 1914. On the one hand, Tenfelde fully confirms Glovka Spencer's theories and, in one chapter of his book which is particularly rich in ideas and material, proves that the mine inspectors in the Ruhr mining industry were largely recruited from the indigenous mining community and that this was scarcely changed by the formalisation of the inspectors' training. On the other hand, he shows that roughly only every sixtieth miner could hope to secure a position as inspector and thus comes to the only initially surprising conclusion that 'the lack of mobility between the classes' was an important factor in the emerging class consciousness of the Ruhr miners. A similar impression is conveyed by the — less numerous — studies which do not deal with opportunities for upward movement in large enterprises and thus provide a more accurate description of the situation of the average worker before 1914. From official surveys on Euskirchen and Cologne one can work out that in the 1830s 4 per cent and 5 per cent of workers' sons became white-collar workers and civil servants respectively and in the 1910s 12 per cent and 13 per cent. Both cases show that the chances of workers' sons moving up into white-collar jobs did increase in the course of the nineteenth century, but on the whole remained unfavourable and the majority of workers' sons became workers in their turn.[8]

In an article in which she published initial results of a study of the machine-building workers in Esslingen between 1846 and 1914, Heilwig Schomerus makes a further important qualification of the pessimistic hypothesis. She arrives at impressive figures for the elite machine-building workers, showing sons of lathemen and locksmiths becoming self-employed or rising into white-collar positions within the railway administration (see Table 3.1). She argues that the favourable internal training facilities and the favourable life-earnings curve, with steady and high earnings from a relatively early age were decisive for these high rates of upward mobility. This is, however, probably a special case, first, because the working and living conditions of the elite machine-building workers were exceptionally favourable to social mobility and, secondly, because the machine-building factory in Esslingen introduced internal training courses at a particularly early stage which seem to have been unusually open. On the broader basis of a whole series of older surveys of the opportunities for occupational and upward mobility among working-class children, Peter Stearns also paints a cautiously optimistic picture. Measured against the expectations of a section of the skilled workers of moving up into the lower middle class, the opportunities for social ascent were disappointing; the opportunities for advancement within the factory to foreman or at least within the working class from unskilled to skilled worker were, on the other hand, quite favourable, at least in large factories. Stearns does not have the actual industrial revolution in mind here but refers above all to the investigations carried out in the early twentieth century.[9]

All in all, research on the opportunities for occupational and upward movement among European and to some extent also American industrial workers during industrialisation presents a pessimistic picture — apart from some very revealing exceptions. Four barriers in particular have been strongly emphasised by research so far: (1) the barrier of capital which, under the conditions of low real income, a high degree of insecurity of employment, a high degree of individual vulnerability to crisis and, therefore, low levels of savings which were difficult to plan, made it extremely difficult for the mass of the workers to raise the capital for a secure business of their own; (2) the barriers of occupational training and school education which allowed above all only a few unskilled workers and their sons to move up into prospering trades and non-manual occupations; (3) the mentality of the early industrial workers which restricted the appreciation and utilisation of career opportunities and the chances of social ascent; (4) the priority of security over the exploitation of opportunities for occupational and upward movement. This priority was necessary since in personal crises such as illness, unemployment, the death of employable members of the family, the loss of accommodation, large numbers of children, and migration, the state provided hardly any social security and traditional institutions like the family, neighbours, self-help organisations and poor relief were insufficient. Undoubtedly, these conditions did not apply to the same extent to all strata of the working class, to all branches of industry or to all regions. Undoubtedly, the educational barriers were not as high and the priority of security not as great for the labour aristocracy since they had a higher, and above all, steadier income, and their living conditions were, therefore, more secure and their education more easily planned. In some regions – such as Esslingen or Berlin – the labour aristocracy obviously made use of these opportunities. It was and remained, however, only a small section of the working class which, in the case of England, has been estimated as 10-15 per cent and was probably no larger in other countries.

Nevertheless, research on the career opportunities and the chances for social ascent among industrial workers is still in its infancy, for a number of crucial questions have not yet been answered:

(1) It is still unclear whether the opportunities for social ascent among workers have changed through and during industrialisation. So far the suspicion that the opportunities for upward movement were more favourable before the industrial revolution has no more been proved right or wrong than has the assumption that the industrial revolution offered better opportunities for social ascent. The results will probably be very varied depending on whether a comparison is made with commercial towns, with proto-industrial areas or with non-industrial, agricultural areas. Previous research has shown very clearly that a one-sided concentration on occupational and upward mobility is too narrowly conceived and that, in addition to the career and work situation, the numerous aspects relating to living conditions and family structure are of great importance. On the basis of the present state of research, it could well be argued that the industrial revolution was not a

'golden age' as far as career chances and opportunities for upward movement are concerned but rather a trough and a period in which there was a particularly strong threat of social descent. A number of factors supported this assumption of a deterioration in opportunities for social ascent among workers: the large growth in population which not only made the planning of careers and of social ascent more difficult, but also intensified competition in the labour market; the increasing capital-intensity of production which, at least in some branches of the economy, raised the capital barrier for those trying to become small-scale industrialists: the increasingly exclusive tie to a working-class occupation which reduced economic and occupational flexibility; the weakening of security in situations of personal crisis since, on the one hand, the family was exposed to increased stress through a large number of children and migration, and on the other hand the traditional charitable institutions and the communal poor relief were overburdened by the increase in poverty. Other factors, which could have favourably influenced the opportunities for occupational and upward mobility among workers, were still largely absent during the industrial revolution: white-collar and civil service occupations, which offered new and often superior opportunities for social ascent to those provided in the traditional lower middle class careers, were still rare. The opportunities for upward movement in retail trade, the expansion of which followed the mass production of clothing and food, did not increase until later. There was hardly any intervention by the state or local government in the sphere of social security which could, even to a limited extent, have relieved private career planning from the pressure imposed by the priority of security and the threat of social descent. A policy of equal opportunity for the lower strata barely existed as an objective let alone as an effective policy. To what extent these factors influenced the change in social mobility is certainly not yet clear. To establish this point the first and most important step would be to carry out investigations of the opportunities for social mobility among the working class over long periods.

(2) Furthermore, too little attention has been paid hitherto to the question of how the channels of social mobility developed. Undoubtedly, the type of investigation which has predominated hitherto – the urban study – has produced important results on occupational mobility rates, on the role of ethnic groups, and on the ascent to home-ownership. Hitherto, however, three crucial factors of social mobility have remained too much in the background: the importance of the work process and the opportunities for mobility within the plant and among

different positions in the plant hierarchy; the distribution of opportunities in the sphere of occupational training and education; and finally, living conditions, i.e. accommodation, medical provision, protection from crime, the family, and the influence of these factors on the planning and opportunities for mobility. All these channels and conditions of mobility cannot be investigated in urban studies. The study of particular firms, and of training, the analysis of particular aspects of living conditions and investigations of social strata and classes would all be promising alternative forms of investigation.

(3) It is still unclear whether European workers during the industrial revolution really did have less favourable opportunities for upward movement than American workers. Up to now this hypothesis could only be documented by positively bold comparisons between individual cities; Tables 3.3 and 3.4 show that there are always some cases which support and other cases which cast doubt on this thesis, and that a general comparison between random American and random European cities leads to severe problems. Much more promising would be comparisons between cities which show similarities in size and growth, economic structure and development, occupational structure and change. More comparisons should be made between the non-modern, non-industrial spheres of American and European society since, in the nineteenth century, the more striking differences may well have lain there; they certainly provoke the most controversial opinions today.

(4) Finally, we still do not know what influence social recruitment and opportunities for mobility had on the class consciousness of workers. Here previous work has tended to indicate the limits of research on social mobility. Social origins, migration and opportunities for social ascent are certainly an important factor in social consciousness and social conflict; in the context of a study of class consciousness, however, they are surely only one dimension, which needs to be examined — alongside the development of the standard of living, the homogeneity of working and living conditions, expectations of working and living conditions, and the communications structures and the political factors such as ideology, political leadership potential, and the degree of repression within the political system.

4 THE DEVELOPMENT OF EQUALITY OF OPPORTUNITY IN THE EDUCATION SECTOR

In the past decade, historians, as well as sociologists and educationalists working in the historical field, have studied the development of educational opportunities more than ever before. The decisive factor in the increase in research on the social history of education was almost invariably the political debate on the equality of educational opportunities which took place during the 1960s, even though the historical dimension did not play a key role in this political debate. Social scientists of different disciplines became increasingly interested in three particular aspects of the social history of education: first, more data and facts were needed on the question of whether inequality of opportunity in education had decreased in the course of the nineteenth and twentieth centuries, or whether the initial impression that this was an area little affected by industrialisation would be confirmed. In many cases, this required tedious statistical work which only a few historians had undertaken. Secondly, there has been much more intensive discussion of the effects of industrialisation on the distribution of educational opportunities. On the one hand, it was suspected that industrialisation required sooner or later the more effective use of the reservoir of talent and thus decreased inequality of opportunity; that, in addition, industrialisation increased educational facilities, widened educational functions, changed educational institutions, lowered the cost of education and thereby produced a somewhat more even distribution of educational opportunities. Against this, on the other hand, it has been pointed out that the industrial revolution destroyed a society in which traditional patronage by the wealthy, patriarchal welfare, charitable foundations and the village community had offered the more intelligent men from the lower stratum quite favourable educational opportunities and that industrialisation, at any rate in its early phase, led to an increase in equality of opportunity. This question too has scarcely been investigated by historical research on education. Thirdly, more work has been done on the effectiveness of educational reforms. Some people suspected that the ineffectiveness of educational policy in the past has been a decisive factor in the inequality of educational opportunity in the present. The earlier educational reforms were either considered to have been too unsystematically planned and implemented or they were regarded above all as capitalist forms of education, which increased productivity but imposed purely middle-class educational institutions and values, and excluded the working class from academic training. Moreover, interest in the historical study of educational reform was particularly strong among non-historians; they saw in it the only possibility of examining the effects of educational policy which were only very slowly becoming visible. In the process, some sociologists went an important step further than most of the historians. They attempted to establish not only whether educational policy altered inequality of opportunity in the access to or during the course of education, but, in addition, whether it had a lasting effect on later career chances. This third aspect also led to new topics, since the older historical research on education, with only a few exceptions, had concentrated on educational ideas, institutions and politicians, but had paid little attention to the historical changes in education which had been going on behind educational theories, legal texts and institutions.

Like the discussion on the trend of social mobility, there are two debates on the history of educational opportunity which are continuing independently of one another. Here too, one of them is concerned with the period of industrialisation. This debate is almost entirely confined to social historians. Parallel to it, there is a discussion about the development of educational opportunities in the twentieth century in which sociologists are the main participants. Both debates concentrate mainly on European countries. Research on the USA, on the other hand, deals very rarely with the historical development of the distribution of opportunities between social strata and classes. Even the revisionist school concentrates above all on the history of educational ideologies, programmes, politicians, and bureaucracies and has hardly ever investigated educational opportunities through methods of quantification. The USA is not, therefore, dealt with in this chapter.

Industrialisation

Discussion in England about the effects of the industrial revolution on educational opportunities appears to have been initiated in 1951 by Nicholas Hans. At any rate, he provided the first empirical evidence for the thesis that the industrial revolution drastically increased inequality of opportunity in academic education. His statistics on the social origins of students at Oxford and Cambridge clearly demonstrate a strong relative decline in the numbers of students from the lower strata between 1750 and 1800. He sees the reason for this in the industrial revolution. The pre-industrial village community, in which talented boys from the lower strata were encouraged by the teacher, the parson and possibly by the lord of the manor, were sent to the grammar school and from there reached university in considerable numbers, disintegrated. In its place emerged, in Hans' view, an involuntarily mobile, socially isolated working class, which, because of its living and working conditions, was incapable of developing independent educational initiatives, and whose upwardly mobile members were blocked by the middle class. Almost simultaneously with Hans, C. Arnold Anderson and M. Schnaper published a study on the social origins and occupational careers of Oxford and Cambridge students between 1752 and 1938. They too came to the conclusion that the number of students from the lower strata at Oxford declined sharply up to 1800, while those at Cambridge at any rate did not increase perceptibly during the eighteenth and nineteenth centuries. They saw the cause of the inequality of opportunity in Oxford and Cambridge in the nineteenth century in the reforms of the 1850s which sharply reduced the possibilities for sons of the lower stratum to win scholarships or make earnings on the side. In an essay written in 1961, which dealt with the public schools between 1800 and 1950, T.W. Bamford also supported this pessimistic view. In the course of the nineteenth century, attendance at these private boarding schools became increasingly a prerequisite for access to the few English universities. The public grammar schools were, by comparison, insignificant. Bamford established that the pupils of the eight most important public schools between 1800 and 1850 were noticeably less likely to come from the lower and middle strata, i.e., from families of domestic servants, artisans, the *petite bourgeoisie* or industrialists. The percentage declined from 50 per cent to 24 per cent. Finally, in 1960 Brian Simon confirmed this pessimistic assessment of the effects of the industrial revolution. Like Anderson and Schnaper, he argued that as a result of the English educational reforms of the 1850s and 1860s – in other words after the real industrial revolution – the educational opportunities of the industrial working class were decisively reduced. He sees the positive aspect of these reforms in the fact that the two important universities, Oxford and Cambridge, were transformed from being religious seminaries into modern universities offering scientific and legal training and were thereby adapted to the requirements of industrialisation. At the same time, however, in his opinion the class character of the English education system imposed itself whereby secondary education was restricted to the aristocracy and the middle class, while the industrial working class were confined to elementary schools. Like Bamford, he sees the growing importance of the private, expensive and therefore exclusive, public schools, and the change in the policy of the charitable foundations, which had previously aimed to encourage the sons of poor families but now distributed their scholarships solely on the basis of merit, as decisive factors. Simon developed his theories on the basis of contemporary reports and protests, but did not possess any representative figures on the actual social origins of secondary school pupils and students.[1]

A different position has been developed in some recent works. In 1969 Sheldon Rothblatt cast doubt on the accuracy of Simon's arguments without, however, being able to put forward any real evidence to the contrary. John Lawson and Harold Silver assessed the educational reforms after 1870 in a positive light because they led to a more open educational system in England. An article by Lawrence Stone on the students at Oxford between 1850 and 1910 opened entirely new perspectives. He fully confirmed the thesis of Hans about the decline in the educational opportunities for members of the lower and lower middle strata in the eighteenth century but puts forward a different interpretation for it. He considers that this increase in inequality of opportunity was already underway in the sixteenth century and not only since the beginning of the industrial revolution. While in the years 1577-9 55 per cent of the students still came from 'plebeian' families, in 1637-9 only 37 per cent, in 1760 only 17 per cent, and in 1810 only 1 per cent still did so. He sees the decisive reason for this development not in the industrial revolution but in the long-term reduction of career prospects for the clergy who were predominantly trained in Oxford and Cambridge until the mid-nineteenth century, in the increasing cost of education, in the progressively more opulent and aristocratic lifestyle of the students and in the progressive reduction since the sixteenth century in the number of scholarships and grants for the sons of poor families, who were displaced by the sons of nobles and of the clergy and not – as Hans's statistics also confirm – by the sons of industrialists. Stone's results relate to Simon's thesis in a similar fashion. Here too, on the one hand, Stone's work confirms it, since according to his surveys the Oxford students between 1870 and 1910 continued to be recruited extremely rarely from working-class families. On the other hand, Stone considers that around 1870 there was a caesura, since in the following decades the number of students from noble families and those of the clergy declined drastically, whereas

Table 4.1: The social status of the students at Oxford University 1577-1880

	Peer baronet and knight		Armiger (esquire)		Gentleman		Higher clergy, clergy, and Drs		Plebeian		Annual Total	Unknown
	Annual No.	%	Annual No.	%	Annual No.	%	Annual No.	%	Annual No.	%		
1577-79	7	3	31	13	60	26	8	3	129	55	235	3
1600-02	11	3	58	19	96	31	15	5	133	42	313	4
1627-29	16	6	26	10	46	17	40	15	137	52	265	0
1637-39	30	7	49	12	123	29	62	15	156	37	420	0
1661-62	14	4	52	14	97	26	59	16	147	40	369	0
1686	16	5	32	10	98	32	63	21	98	32	307	0
1711	15	5	45	14	108	33	69	21	87	27	324	0
1735-36	13	5	62	24	66	26	47	18	70	27	258	0
1760-61	10	5	59	29	56	28	43	21	35	17	203	1
1785-86	11	5	72	30	77	32	55	23	23	10	238	0
1810	23	7	129	40	74	23	94	29	4	1	324	0
1835	15	4	189	51	76	21	89	24	1	0	370	0
1860	13	3	135	34	126	32	120	31	0	0	394	0
1885	17	2	242	33	289	39	193	26	1	0	742	0

Source: L. Stone 'The Size and Composition of the Oxford Student Body 1580-1909,' in L. Stone (ed.), *The University in Society*, vol. 1 (Princeton, 1974), p. 93.

Table 4.2: The social origins of students at Oxford University 1870-1910 (per cent)

	1870	1891	1910
Knights, baronets and peers	2)	1)	1)
Esquires and gentlemen	36)	16)	8)
JPs and MPs	2) 40	1) 21	0) 15
Landowners and farmers	0)	3)	6)
Clergy	28	24	17
Lawyers	7)	12)	9)
Doctors	5)	4)	6)
Teachers	1)	2)	6)
Architects	0) 21	0) 27	0) 31
Civil Servants	1)	3)	5)
Armed forces and police	5)	4)	4)
Artists and publishers	2)	2)	1)
Industrialists and businessmen	7	19	21
Tradesmen, shopkeepers and agents	2)	6)	7)
Secretaries and clerks	0) 2	2) 8	2) 9
Working class	0)	0)	1)
Unknown	2	1	5
Total in Sample	418	669	1030

Source: Stone, 'The Size and Composition of the Oxford Student Body, 1580-1909', p. 103.

students from the families of industrialists underwent a considerable increase and those from lower middle-class families a slight increase (see Table 4.2). Thus, in Stone's view, the opportunities for social ascent via university education increased. In his view, this resulted from the considerable reduction in the cost of education, in the aristocratic life-style of the students and from an expansion in student numbers which was unique in the history of Oxford and which was produced by the strong demand for people with a university education – particularly in the British colonial administration – and by the modernisation of the University of Oxford referred to by Simon.[2] In general, Stone largely confirms the pessimistic thesis of Hans and Simon concerning the development of educational opportunities for the pre-industrial lower strata and the industrial workers during the eighteenth and nineteenth centuries. In his view, however, the decisive factors are not the destruction of an open, pre-industrial society and an educational policy geared to capitalist interests, but other factors which determined the cost of education and the demand for university graduates, such as the church, the civil service, the student subculture and the function of universities.

There are only a few studies of educational opportunities in Germany during its industrialisation. They do not link up directly with the English discussion, but pose similar questions. After the war, Wolfgang Zorn was the first person to pursue historical research on the question of equality of opportunity in the educational field. In 1964, on the basis of numerous scattered surveys, he was able to show that although the industrial revolution altered the social origins of students, it did not lead to a reduction in inequality of opportunity and, if anything, led to a deterioration in the already minimal educational opportunities of the lower strata. In his view the neo-humanistic educational policy of the post-Napoleonic period of reaction, the designation of the *Abitur* (graduation from secondary education) as a compulsory qualification for university students, and the privileged position given to the classical *Gymnasium* (grammar school) actually exacerbated the unequal distribution of educational opportunities. In 1975, Konrad Jarausch studied the social origins of students at five German universities during the first half of the nineteenth century — Heidelberg, Göttingen, Tübingen, Erlangen and Kiel — which, in his opinion, provided a representative picture for the area of the later German Reich. Jarausch established that there was an increase in inequality of opportunity at the beginning of the industrial revolution. Unlike the English case, it was not the lower strata which were affected, which in any case had, around 1800, very limited academic opportunities, but rather the lower middle class. But according to Jarausch's statistics this was not a long-term trend, but a sudden development during the 1840s, which Jarausch (like Stone) attributed not to industrialisation, but to the irregularity of economic growth during this decade and to the decline in the number of posts for university graduates in the civil service. It is possible that the negative effects of the humanistic educational policy forecast by Zorn were making themselves felt in this development. Finally, in 1975, Peter Lundgreen used the example of the Berlin *Gewerbeinstitut* to investigate the opportunities for non-academic training of engineers between 1820 and 1870, which have been largely neglected by researchers. He too argues that, despite the growing demand for engineers during the industrial revolution, equality of opportunity at the *Gewerbeinstitut* did not improve at all, but actually deteriorated. Like Zorn, Lundgreen explains this mainly in terms of education policy: the restriction of scholarships at the *Gewerbeinstitut* as a reaction to the Revolution of 1848, and the effects of the conservative educational policy during the post-Napoleonic period of reaction which pushed the *Gewerbeinstitut* into the trend towards academicism. These studies are unanimous in their negative assessment of the development of equality of opportunity during the industrialisation before 1870. They differ, however, from Nicholas Hans and Brian Simon in that they do not regard industrialisation as the reason for the unequal distribution of educational opportunities but, above all, the educational policy at the time. This, in turn, is interpreted not as capitalist education policy but rather as the reaction of a traditional elite to the social consequences of industrialisation. It is only recently that a more optimistic assessment appeared to be emerging as well, above all with reference to the Prussian *Gymnasium* in the pre-March period. Apart from the work of Detlev K. Müller, which will have to be dealt with later, this view has been put forward by Margret Kraul in a short preview of a longer article not yet published. Kraul uses the case of the secondary schools in Minden to show that pupils from the middle and lower middle class predominated, although the upper middle class clearly increased their proportion among *Abitur* students. Kraul comes to the specific conclusion that the secondary schools in pre-March Prussia were – subject to confirmation by later case studies – 'more democratic and meritocratic rather than aristocratic, socially elite schools'.

The development of equality of opportunity in academic education after 1870 has also scarcely been investigated. Fritz Ringer published some brief reflections on this subject in 1969, which he intends to expand and treat comparatively in the near future. From these, it emerges that inequality of opportunity before the First World War decreased in a similar fashion and to a similar extent as in Britain at the time. The proportion of students with a graduate family background declined. Families of landowners, clergy and higher civil servants, whose sons traditionally attended universities were less strongly represented. Not only were they replaced by more sons of industrialists, but facilities for academic education improved considerably for students from the *petite bourgoisie* and from the families of middle-ranking civil servants. At the same time, this change had similar limitations as in Britain. The children of workers and of peasants, but also the children of white-collar employees, were largely excluded from the universities and scarcely benefitted from the expansion of university education. Apart from the development of the standard of living and of the cost of education, and the barriers provided by the student subculture, Ringer believes that, in the period after 1870, the educational institutions were responsible for this, i.e., the institutional separation of elementary education and secondary education, which made the transition to secondary education and to the universities barely feasible for pupils from elementary schools, and almost completely prevented the encouragement of talent independent of class considerations. The curriculum of the classical *Gymnasium*, from which the majority of students came, reinforced these barriers. Unlike Simon, Ringer regards the German educational system which, like that of Britain, impeded access to secondary education, not as a consequence of the capitalist form of industrial revolution but, conversely, as a traditional pre-industrial structure which was preserved in Germany longer than in other countries. He sees the socially somewhat more open recruitment of university students during the later period of the Second Reich not as the result of a planned democratisation of education, but as the adaptation of pre-industrial classes such as tradesmen, artisans and civil servants to an industrial society in which education had a particularly high social status and was, therefore, an important avenue of social advancement. In a hitherto unpublished paper, Konrad Jarausch assesses the extensive published material on the origins of Prussian, Saxon and Württemberg students in more detail. For the period between 1870 and 1914 he, like Ringer, finds a limited opening up of the universities, a relative decrease in students from the families of graduates and a relative increase in students from the propertied middle class and the non-independent middle class, from teachers' families, non-graduate civil servants and white-collar employees. Jarausch stresses, however, that the situation varied considerably between the faculties and that the universities remained as inaccessible as ever for the growing number of industrial workers. According to Jarausch, the decisive factors in this limited change were: the beginnings of the secular growth in student numbers, the recognition of the *Realabschluss* (modern secondary education) as a qualification for admission to university and, finally, the expansion of white-collar and civil service occupations. In one of the few investigations involving a comparison, Jürgen Kocka attempts to explain the relative openness of German secondary schools and universities compared with the English universities of the late nineteenth century (Oxford and Cambridge). In his view, the decisive reason for this is the stronger motivation of the German lower middle class, above all of the non-graduate civil servants and independent artisans towards a university education for their sons. This stronger motivation was determined by two traditional traits of Imperial German society: first, by the traditionally high social prestige of university education in Germany, closely linked with bureaucratic traditions; secondly, by the more rigid social hierarchy and lower career mobility in Germany which, in Kocka's opinion, fostered stronger expectations from the secondary and university education of their sons. Thus, Kocka, like Ringer, does not regard the relatively broad social background of the pupils and students in Germany as an indication of a democratised school system. Ringer's and Jarausch's theories are also supported by the study by Hartmut Titze, who evaluated some of the available data on the distribution of opportunities at *Gymnasien* – above all a survey of Barmen done in 1905. Titze also shows that the chances of entry into *Gymnasien* were extremely small for workers' children and that, moreover, the proportion of pupils from the *petite bourgeoisie*, from white-collar employees', and from workers' families was progressively reduced in the senior classes in the schools. Titze argues that education and wealth were decisive for access to secondary schools. The marked differences within the rather vaguely defined group 'property and education' (*Besitz und Bildung*), the specific economic and institutional reasons for the inequality of opportunity in the Second Reich and the changes which affected them are made less clear than in the studies of Ringer and Jarausch. Finally, in a study of the change in the structure of the German school system during the nineteenth century, Detlev K. Müller reaches perhaps the most pessimistic assessment of the period after 1870. In his view, the German school developed from a differentiated common school in the pre-March period into a vertically structured, exclusive elite school system in the 1880s, from an easily accessible avenue of upward mobility into a type of school whose primary function was to provide a means for the university-educated bourgeoisie to bequeath status, and which only admitted highly talented sons of the lower middle and lower strata to secondary education. With the aid of numerous documents, Müller proves that educational policy, especially in the 1880s, was geared to a reduction in the educational opportunities of the lower middle class, and sees the educated bourgeoisie and the *Gymnasium* teachers as the main beneficiaries of this policy. Müller's statistical material on the case of Berlin does not, however, demonstrate that this policy of reduced educational opportunities was very successful, but supports Ringer's and Jarausch's thesis that the number of pupils taking the *Abitur* rapidly increased and that the proportion of these pupils from the lower middle class did not decrease. The value of Müller's work, therefore, – as Peter Lundgreen also suggests in a detailed discussion of it – lies above all in demonstrating the contradiction between the elitist education policy and the demand for university graduates in the Second Reich.[3]

In recent years, a number of works have also appeared on developments in France, which have tended to concentrate on the effects of educational reforms and, to a lesser extent, on the effects of industrialisation on the distribution of educational opportunities. As was shown in the discussion on the connexion between the industrial revolution and equality of opportunities in the educational sector in England, it is important to consider the eighteenth-century background. In this context, H. Chisick investigated secondary schools (*collèges*) in Paris during the last decades before the French Revolution. The middle class predominated even among the scholarship pupils, i.e.; pupils from the families of businessmen, higher civil servants, *rentiers* and professional men. Pupils from the lower strata were virtually excluded from scholarships and for that reason were probably extremely rare among the other students. Wilhelm Frijhoff and Dominique Julia, who investigated the distribution of opportunities at three other pre-revolutionary secondary schools outside Paris (Avallon, Gisors and Condom) came to similar conclusions. Despite the extraordinarily wide differences between the *collèges*, they seem to have in common the fact that the lower strata had virtually no opportunity of access to secondary education and they came, if at all, from the elite of the peasantry and the artisans. Frijhoff and Julia even gained the impression that the amount of secondary education began to diminish in the pre-revolutionary period and, at the same time, inequality of opportunity began to increase. If the results of these two investigations are applicable to other French *collèges* and universities in general, then the opportunities for university education among the lower classes would have been like those in Germany – extremely poor even at the beginning of the industrial revolution – and could hardly have deteriorated further as a result of it.

A number of studies have appeared recently on secondary education after the French Revolution which, in contrast to the literature on England and Germany, contain mainly optimistic assessments. Robert Anderson investigated the French state secondary schools. He regards the French secondary school system in the nineteenth century as open and democratic and explains this above all in terms of the effects of the French Revolution and of the Napoleonic era. The education policy in this period led, broadly speaking, to a predominance of the middle class and lower middle class in the French secondary schools since the school fees were low, the schools widely scattered geographically, admission determined solely on the basis of merit and the French upper class sent their sons to expensive and exclusive Catholic private schools.

Anderson's positive assessment is, however, to a large extent based on the fact that he does not draw any comparisons with the social origins of the secondary schools in pre-revolutionary France or in other European countries during the nineteenth century and that he does not include the educational opportunities of the lower classes in his assessment. The optimism expressed in the other studies of developments in France is considerably more low-key. C.R. Day investigated the *enseignement secondaire spécial*, a special branch of French secondary education founded in 1865, which was geared much more to the requirements of industry and offered tuition above all in the applied sciences and technology in place of the classics. It was modelled on the Swiss and German *Realschule*. This branch of French secondary education offered unusually favourable educational opportunities to the *petite bourgeoisie*, to farmers and the labour elite. Day does not, however, consider the effect on occupational opportunities as very great. Attendance at these schools ensured access to middle ranking posts in the civil service and in business for the sons of farmers and of the *petite bourgeoisie*, but did not offer opportunities of moving up into the middle class. Patrick Harrigan analysed a rare source, a questionnaire issued by the French Minister of Education in 1864-65 on the social origins and later higher education of French grammar school pupils. He too does not regard the French secondary schools and the *grandes écoles* as purely upper-class institutions. At the military academies and in the traditional courses such as law and medicine, the students from the traditional upper class, from the families of lawyers, *rentiers* and *propriétaires* largely predominated. On the other hand, sons of businessmen and of the *petite bourgeoisie* did gain access to courses of study such as those at the École Polytechnique and the École Centrale, which were established after the collapse of the *ancien régime* and from which the top civil servants and big industrialists emerged. Although this system of education remained largely inaccessible to workers' and farmers' children for financial reasons, it did, in Harrigan's view, constitute an important avenue for upward mobility for the *petite bourgeoisie*. Harrigan, like Anderson, does not, however, answer the question of how opportunities in secondary and higher education in France have changed in the long run. Hitherto, this question has only been dealt with by a group round Maurice Lévy-Leboyer, which investigated the *grandes écoles* in the nineteenth and twentieth centuries. The results which have been published so far show a development of educational opportunities quite similar to that in England and Germany. It was only in the second phase of industrialisation, after about 1890, that equality of opportunity at several of these *grandes écoles* changed in favour of students from the families of white-collar employees, farmers and above all the *petite bourgeoisie*. Here, too, the expansion of student numbers was decisive, which Lévy-Leboyer explains in terms of the phase of prosperity before the First World War and the growing demand for university graduates.[4]

The development of educational opportunities in Scotland appears to be in sharp contrast to the countries discussed above. M. Mathew made use of the remarkably informative matriculation lists of Glasgow University and investigated the regional and social origins of the students and their occupations between 1740 and 1840, i.e., in the preparatory phase of the industrial revolution in Scotland. Mathew established that at this university, which was mainly attended by Scots, equality of opportunity improved considerably. The proportion of sons of noblemen and big landowners fell drastically; their places were filled above all by sons of the working class, i.e. from the families of skilled and artisanal workers, whose proportion rose to 25 per cent. The educational opportunities for farmers' sons were also considerably greater than in the rest of Europe; their proportion of the student numbers did fall from 25 per cent to 15 per cent, which was, however, caused by changes in the social structure and remained at an unusually high level. Thus, in 1800, there was at the University of Glasgow a degree of equality of opportunity which has only rarely been achieved in modern West European universities. Mathew considers that there were several reasons for this Scottish situation. In the first place, the sons of the Scottish nobility and big landowners moved to English secondary schools and universities because they appeared to provide a better guarantee of exclusiveness. Secondly, the highly developed Scottish school system, which had been established by the Presbyterian church, made a systematic and successful attempt to achieve a maximum of equality of educational opportunity. Thirdly, the educational costs were low in Glasgow because the fees were low, accommodation and the possibility of earning money on the side were readily available and scholarships were awarded frequently. Mathew does not, however, provide an answer to the question of whether employment vacancies for graduates increased or of how the highly developed Scottish school system was financed in such a relatively poor country. Mathew only touches on the effects of the real industrial revolution on educational opportunities because to deal with this he would need to go further into the nineteenth century, since craft journeymen and masters were impoverished by technological change and the cost of education in

Glasgow increased sharply. According to Mathew's observations, the students appear to have only rarely come from the new urban proletariat.[5]

Overall, the opportunities for university education in Western Europe during the industrial revolution improved for only a small section of society – the *petite bourgeoisie*. Moreover, this shift in opportunities only began when the demand for graduates in industry and the civil service increased and the secular expansion in student numbers, which has continued up to the present day, began. It is undisputed that, by contrast, the workers, but also the farmers and, to a lesser extent, the lower white-collar employees were everywhere virtually excluded from this expanding branch of education. The decisive factors here are likely to have been: first, the scissors effect which existed between living standards and the cost of education, which unfortunately has only rarely been investigated. Secondly, there was either no effective scholarship system, or the scholarship systems which had existed hitherto lost their compensating effect, which had been geared to helping impecunious pupils, and did not expand to the same extent as did secondary education. Thirdly, and finally, in contrast to the USA, secondary education in most of the European countries was separated off institutionally from elementary education, which acquired the task of making the mass of the population literate. Almost insuperable barriers arose between the elementary and the secondary schools which virtually excluded any systematic attempt to encourage the talented sons of working-class, peasant, and also white-collar families. Thus, despite considerable differences in the institutions of secondary and higher education, a school system emerged in Europe which was geared to class barriers, in which above all the working class was pushed into a cul-de-sac of elementary education, and secondary education was reserved for the nobility and the *haute bourgeoisie* and the professional middle class and, when it was gradually made more accessible, it was almost exclusively the *petite bourgeoisie* who benefitted. Whether, in addition, the educational opportunities of those in the lower strata were significantly diminished by the industrial revolution has not yet been proved. In the first place, in England their educational chances had begun to deteriorate drastically long before the industrial revolution, and in Germany and France appear to have been or to have become extremely limited before the industrial revolution. Secondly, this thesis has tended to neglect the perspective of the lower strata. The numbers of students were very small in relation to the number of young people from the lower strata as a whole. Even drastic alterations to the equality of opportunity within secondary education, whose numbers of pupils were (in contrast to the present day) in any case very limited, were hardly noticeable in either a negative or a positive sense as far as the lower strata were concerned. It is certainly important for the study of social history in the nineteenth century for the whole of education and vocational training to be included in future in the debate on the effects of industrialisation on educational opportunities.

The Twentieth Century

Discussion of the history of educational opportunities in the twentieth century concentrates more on educational reforms and their effects on equality of opportunity. Here too, British educational history has been particularly thoroughly investigated, whereas developments in Germany and above all those in France and the USA have been researched a good deal less.[6]

Hitherto, the Education Act of 1944, which improved access to secondary education and reduced the cost of education for the pupils involved, has been at the centre of British research. In a retrospective investigation of two selected school districts, J.E. Floud, A.H. Halsey and F.M. Martin reached a favourable assessment of the effects of these reforms – with a few reservations. After the school reform of 1902 had, in the opinion of these researchers, already altered the social structure of the secondary schools and facilitated access for the lower middle class, particularly for white-collar workers, the reforms of 1944 provided access to this level of the school system above all for the children of skilled workers. Ability tests showed, according to the interpretation of this group of researchers, that all those children who were sufficiently talented attended secondary schools and, as a result, there was an optimum distribution of opportunities in the education sector in post-war Britain. Floud, Halsey and Martin did, however, make two reservations. In the first place, they emphasised that the results of intelligence tests are strongly influenced by social factors, in their case by the size of family. Secondly, inequality of opportunity was not removed in the senior classes in the secondary schools. They explain this not in terms of economic barriers or of hostility towards education on the part of working-class parents, but on the basis of the cultural gap which exists between the British working class and the secondary schools as institutions of the middle class, and the lack of cooperation between parents and schools. In an essay published in 1964, two other British sociologists, Alan Little and John Westergaard, made a less positive assessment of the effects of the Education Act of 1944, and for two reasons in particular. They did not dispute the fact that more secondary school pupils came from working-class families. They showed, however, that the proportion of secondary school pupils among the sons and daughters of the upper and middle strata increased much more rapidly than among the children of the working class. Secondly, they showed that equality of opportunity for working-class children only improved in relation to access to secondary schools, whereas access to universities remained the same. Thus, the effects of the Education Act were restricted to the secondary schools and did not alter the distribution of opportunities in higher education let alone in graduate careers. They concluded that the Education Act of 1944 had not gone far enough, that the expensive and, therefore, exclusive private public schools continued largely to determine access to the universities and that the regional distribution of secondary schools was too uneven and there were too few of them. Both Jean Floud and A.H. Halsey later accepted the conclusions of Little and Westergaard in separate publications. Halsey, too, now argued that while children from all social strata were increasingly educated at universities, nevertheless the middle class had benefitted disproportionately from the expansion of student numbers, while in his opinion the chances of access for the children of unskilled workers had actually deteriorated.[7]

There has been much less work on the historical development of the distribution of opportunities in French secondary schools during the twentieth century. Hitherto, there have been mainly only incidental comments. Christiane Peyre, who investigated access to French secondary schools in 1959, came to the conclusion like Floud, Halsey and Martin and in contrast to what we know of Germany, that the opportunities for access had improved (see Table 4.2). Between 1936 and 1944 the percentage of white-collar employees', artisans', and workers' children increased from 9 per cent to 31 per cent, the percentage of workers' children alone from 3 per cent to 14 per cent. After that, however, the percentage of this group stagnated or even decreased slightly. Peyre found no explanation for this dramatic change. Like the British sociologists referred to above, however, she found that the percentage of pupils from these social groups continued to be considerably lower in the senior classes of grammar schools. As far as access to universities during the 1960s is concerned, a research paper by Jane Marceau on the distribution of opportunities in the French system of

Table 4.3: The social origins of French secondary school pupils 1936-57 (per cent)

	1936-37 (1)	1943-44 (2)	1946-47 (3)	1951-52 (4)	1956-57 (5)
Professions	11	7	7	8	9
Businessmen	25	14	17	14	12
Civil servants, officers	29	24	26	26	26
White-collar employees	20	19	17	19	21
Artisans	4	10	10	9	8
Farmers	2	8	9	7	7
Workers	3	14	12	13	12
Others	6	3	3	4	4
Total	100	100	100	100	100
Number in sample	28,806	49,128	57,104	65,548	104,751

Source: C. Peyre 'L.Origine sociale des élèves de l'enseignement secondaire en France' in P. Naville (ed.), *Ecole et Societé* (Paris, 1958) p. 10.

education and its effect on social mobility reveals that — again in contrast to the Federal Republic at that time — the percentage of students from working-class families clearly increased from 5 to 10 per cent. Marceau also takes a sceptical view of this shift since, first, the increase in students from working-class families was concentrated in the natural sciences and the arts subjects in which career prospects were particularly unfavourable. Secondly, Marceau gained the general impression that the French educational system was unable to break through the barriers to mobility in French society but merely reproduced them. Pierre Bourdieu, who has undertaken the most thorough investigation of the distribution of opportunities in the French education system during the past two decades, also produced very unfavourable estimates. The enormous expansion in secondary education which in France produced an increase in the percentage of secondary school pupils between 1950/1 and 1967/8 from 11.5 per cent to 28.3 per cent per year in his view drastically increased the rate of access to secondary schools for all social groups and classes (see Table 4.4). At the same time, the secondary school played a much more important role in the distribution of career opportunities mainly because, with the replacement of proprietors by managers, with the decline in the *petite bourgeoisie* and peasantry and with the expansion in the number of white-collar employees and of dependent careers for graduates, educational qualifications became more and more important for access to better paid, more respected and influential occupations. As a result, the pressure of competition in secondary schools increased; in Bourdieu's

Table 4.4: The rate of secondary school attendance of 16-18 year olds in France 1954-68 (per cent)

	1954 (1)	1962 (2)	1968 (3)
Agricultural wage earners	6.0	23.3	29.7
Agricultural employers	7.5	22.5	36.8
Workers	16.3	26.1	35.4
Entrepreneurs in commerce and industry	30.0	45.0	51.7
White-collar employees	34.9	47.0	54.3
'Cadres moyen'	42.6	71.0	74.6
Supervisory white-collar employees, professions	59.3	87.0	100.0

Source: P. Bourdieu, 'Les stratégies de reconversion. Les classes sociales et la système d'enseignement', *Social Science Information*, 12 (1973), p. 110.

view they became the main area of conflict between social classes over the surrender of economic, social and cultural privileges and positions of power – a conflict in which, as Bourdieu shows in the case of France, the families of occupants of highly qualified, highly paid and prestigious positions come out on top.

Significantly, research on the history of opportunities in the sphere of academic education during the twentieth century in Germany has hitherto dealt not so much with the effectiveness of educational reforms as with missed opportunities for reform. Interest has been focused on two phases of change: the early years of the Weimar Republic and the immediate post-war period after 1945. Moreover, research on the establishment of National Socialist rule has also dealt incidentally with the development of equality of opportunity in secondary education between the seizure of power and the Second World War.

It is not disputed that during the first years of the Weimar Republic significant attempts were made to reform access to secondary education. The introduction of a uniform system of primary schools common to all pupils up to the age of ten, the improvement of secondary education for girls, trials with new arrangements for transfer from primary to secondary schools, the beginnings of centralised scholarship programmes for students in higher education, high levels of investment in education and a rapid expansion in secondary and higher education represented a start which was capable of being developed further. These changes had, however, no appreciable effect on the distribution of opportunities at the universities (See Table 4.5). These attempts at reform were already seriously restricted as a result of the change in the political climate which occurred in the early 1920s, as Hildegard

Milberg showed using the example of Hamburg. Moreover, the political priorities of the reforming parties in the Weimar Republic, the fact that a parliamentary system only existed for a short time, and the Great Depression created exceptionally unfavourable conditions for school and university reforms orientated towards more equality of opportunity.

Research on the effects of National Socialist school and university policies on the distribution of educational opportunities has been almost unanimous in its negative assessment. The drastic cuts in education spending considerably restricted educational facilities. The secondary schools remained virtually untouched as regards their institutional structure and the payment of fees. Special schools such as the Napola and the Adolf Hitler Schools were attended by a slightly higher percentage of workers' children than the average *Gymnasium* but the difference remained marginal. The partial removal of the *Abitur* as a qualification for university entrance in the so-called *Langemarck Studium*, which – as David Schoenbaum estimated – was only taken up by a tiny percentage of 0.14 per cent of students, played an insignificant role. Moreover, all innovations in educational policy served an instrumental function for National Socialist rule rather than as an instrument for abolishing inequality of opportunity. The reduction in educational opportunity had a particularly marked effect on women. At least up until the shortage of qualified workers, which began about 1936, places for women at universities were reduced even more than for men. On the whole, the Nazi period must be regarded as a significant factor in the relative backwardness of German or rather West German secondary and higher education since, to begin with, in other countries during this period secondary schools were being reformed or there was considerably higher investment in the educational sector so that Germany fell behind both in reforms and in investment. Secondly the after effects of the Nazi period in Germany absorbed to a considerable extent educational energies which might conceivably have been used for an effective continuation of the Weimar reforms, but which instead, under the prevailing conditions had to be devoted to the reconstruction of educational institutions, the retraining of teachers and the democratic reorientation of the curricula.

As far as school and university policies in the Western zones and in the early phase of the Federal Republic are concerned, these years are also regarded more or less unanimously as a period when the opportunity for continuing the Weimar reforms was missed. Despite proposals by the American administration, which based its policies on the more

Table 4.5: The social origins of students at Universities in Germany and the Federal Republic 1902-1960 (per cent)

Father's occupation	Prussia 1902-1903 (1)	Ger. 1911-1913 (2)	Ger. 1924-1925 (3)	Ger. 1931 (4)	Ger. 1941 (5)	Fed. Rep. 1951-1952 (6)	Fed. Rep. 1959-1960 (7)
High rank civil servants	16	16	17	14	18	15	17
Professions	5	5	9	6	9	9	10
Officers	1	1	1	2	2	1	1
Big Landowners	2	2	2	1			
Businessmen	10	15	14	12	11	13	14
Self-employed artisans				15	12	13	10
Retailers	24	19	17	3	4	5	4
Farmers	9	9	7	28	23	22	17
Middle rank civil servants	23	24	24	6	10	15	19
Middle and low rank employees	3	3	7	3	3		
Low rank civil servants			2	2			
Small peasants				2	3	4	5
Workers		3	2	2	5	3	3
Others or no information	6	2	0[b]	6			
Total	100	100	100	100	100	100	100
Number in sample	16 467	39 984	62 694	125 072	43 000	102 097	155 228
Upper middle class		39	43	35	36[a]	38	42
Lower middle class		55	55	52	58[a]	55	50
Lower class		4	4	4	4[a]	4	5
Employers		50	49	37	42[a]	40	38
Wage and salary earners		31	28	41	38[a]	41	41

a1939.
b0 = less than 0.45%.
Source: H. Kaelble, 'Chancenungleichheit und akademische Ausbildung, 1910-1960', *Geschichte und Gesellschaft*, 1 (1975), p. 124ff.

modern American school system, despite initiatives from teachers'
associations and trade unions, despite drastic reforms in some federal
states such as Schleswig-Holstein and Berlin, the opportunities for
modernisation and for introducing greater accessibility into secondary
education were not used; some reforms were even modified, as Marion
Klewitz has demonstrated for Berlin. Around 1960, the distribution of
opportunities at the universities was − after taking into account the
change in the occupational structure − still the same as in the latter
part of the Second Reich (see Table 4.5), had even deteriorated for
working-class children at secondary schools, and thus lagged far behind
comparable countries such as the USA, Great Britain, or Sweden.[8]
Only the late 1960s and early 1970s brought marked changes in the
social origins of students in the Federal Republic. The proportion of
working-class children between 1960 and 1975 rose from 5 per cent to
13 per cent. Since the number of students simultaneously increased
from around 207,000 to *c.* 798,000 the number of working-class
children was multiplied by ten.[9] That is undoubtedly the most marked
reduction in the inequality of opportunity in the history of Germany
and West Germany, respectively, during the twentieth century, even if
comparisons with countries at a similar stage of economic development
and with similar political structures demonstrate that the possibilities
of achieving equality of opportunity have by no means been exhausted.
Among the decisive reasons for this development were: the abolition
of school fees, the introduction of a means-tested system of scholarships, the change in the educational motivation of parents as a result
of the educational debate during the 1960s, the expansion of the
secondary school system and of the academic education sector in
general, the improved geographical location of universities and easier
access to secondary and university education for those who had not
passed the *Abitur*. There should, however, be a more thorough investigation into the question of which of these many factors played a key
role and whether the reduction in equality of opportunity in academic
education affected the inequality of opportunity in those careers
requiring academic qualifications. An assessment which was made by
Walter Müller and Karl Ulrich Mayer in 1976 refers to the change in the
social structure of the students and the expansion of education, but
comes to the sceptical conclusion that these educational changes had
at most no effect on the distribution of career opportunities.[10]

The two debates on the effects of industrialisation on educational
opportunities and on educational policy in the twentieth century have
clarified the development of equality of opportunity in the educa-

tional sector. At the same time, one cannot ignore the shortcomings of this new social history of education. The most serious flaw is undoubtedly the concentration on secondary schools and universities and the almost complete lack of interest in the distribution of opportunities outside the fields of secondary and higher education. This bias is particularly significant for developments in social mobility because it is only recently that university education has been essential for access to a considerable number of jobs. If the distribution of educational opportunities had any impact on social mobility during the nineteenth and early twentieth centuries, then it did so above all through training acquired outside secondary schools and universities. This research bias is undoubtedly connected with the fact that the political debate in the 1960s was concerned almost exclusively with the universities. Secondly, in the history of educational reform there is an almost complete dearth of investigations of the decision-making process in relation to particular reforms or abortive reforms. In most cases, no real attempt has been made to analyse which interests were in favour of and which opposed reforms, how the teachers' organisations, the parents' associations, the churches, socialist, liberal and conservative parties, trade unions, and employers' associations all reacted, and how they influenced the decision-making process, what role was played by the proposals of academic experts and what influence was exerted by those who were affected − whether of the privileged or deprived social strata. A third weakness of the existing research has been that educational research oriented towards the social history of equality of opportunity between social strata and classes has concentrated mainly on Europe. Even American social historians have been more preoccupied with Europe than with the USA. This is unfortunate because equality of opportunity in the American educational system must have changed during the twentieth century to an unprecedented degree and thus could provide an interesting comparison with Europe. An important reason for the lack of American studies is undoubtedly the fact that university education was much more important for access to well-paid and prestigious careers in the nineteenth and twentieth centuries in Europe than in the USA. Thus, it was not only present-day historians who found studies of European universities more appealing. In addition, the highly decentralised university system in the USA has complicated the task of the historian, who can hardly do more than study a single unrepresentative university, whereas in Prussia and Germany statistical data have been compiled on the social origins of all students for almost a century. A fourth significant flaw is the unwillingness of most historians to tackle the question of how changes in educational opportunities have affected social mobility. In not one country has there been a study of whether the considerable improvement in the opportunities for academic education among the lower middle class at the end of the nineteenth and the early twentieth century also had the effect of improving the career opportunities of this social group, or whether the sons of the middle class and the upper class continued to have much better career opportunities after graduation. It remains to be discovered whether the graduates from the lower middle class did not in fact follow the same careers as their fathers despite their degrees, or how far and since when higher education really opened up a multitude of new career opportunities. The failure to pursue this question is mainly the result of a lack of suitable sources. But the studies of Mathew and Harrigan show that there are some instances in which this question can be resolved. Fifthly and finally, there have been no historical comparisons. The variety of educational systems and the differences in the functions and in the assessment of education may appear discouraging; but the use of historical comparisons is undoubtedly one of the best methods of tracing historical causes of inequality of opportunity in the educational sector.[11]

5 THE RECRUITMENT OF ELITES

In contrast to those fields of historical research into social mobility which have been dealt with so far, the recruitment of elites is by no means a new theme introduced in recent years or, indeed, even in the postwar period. Innumerable studies of the social origins of elites have been written since the beginning of the twentieth century. Surprisingly, however, these studies have only rarely dealt with the question which, above all, concerns present-day research on the history of social mobility, namely the question of historical changes in the recruitment of elites. They have dealt mainly with the recruitment of an elite at a particular historical moment. This is all the more surprising because in no other area of historical research on social mobility have concepts of historical change been developed and discussed so intensively over such a long period. Max Weber's concept of the transition from amateur to professional politician, Robert Michels's iron law of oligarchy, Joseph Schumpeter's idea of the end of the classic entrepreneur who was recruited from every social group and of the emergence of an exclusive managerial class — all these represent concepts which have been developed and which await adoption, empirical application and further development by historians. In this field too, it was sociologists and political scientists who began the historical research: Reinhard Bendix in the USA, Mattei Dogan in France, W.L. Guttsman in Great Britain, and Wolfgang Zapf in the German Federal Republic.

Instead of giving a tedious survey of innumerable detailed studies of the recruitment of historical elites, this research report intends to concentrate on the work dealing with long-term historical changes in the recruitment of elites, and to provide an answer to the question whether or not elites have become more open or more exclusive since the industrial revolution and whether upward mobility was facilitated or made more difficult as a result. The only two elites to be dealt with will be those on which extensive research has already been carried out: the economic elite and the political elite. The question of how top positions in the military, church and cultural spheres were filled has hitherto been seriously neglected. John A. Armstrong has only recently published a survey on the administrative elite.[1]

The Business Elite

During the past fifteen years or so — with the exception of the last few years — there has been very little historical investigation of the recruitment of businessmen; there was, however, a good deal of research on this topic in the fields of sociology and economic history during the late 1940s and the 1950s. The sociological research was related above all to the question of equality of opportunity and the hardening of class distinctions in modern industrial society, and to the questions of the quality of management and the bureaucratisation of large-scale enterprises. Major sociologists of the immediate postwar period such as Bendix, Warner and Mills dealt with these problems through empirical investigations. It is characteristic of this period of sociological research that it had a marked historical slant, while numerous later sociological studies of economic elites — such as those in recent years on businessmen in the German Federal Republic or in France — have almost completely abandoned the historical perspective. Moreover, the majority of sociological research was carried out in the USA. In Europe before 1960, only one important study of this kind had been written — on the history of British businessmen. In the field of economic history there is a long tradition of research on the business elite. Here too, however, it was only after the Second World War that this developed from a series of impressionistic observations into investigations using methods of quantification, and it was based partly on the question of capital accumulation, a standard topic of economic history, and partly on interest in entrepreneurial attitudes as a factor in economic growth, which developed under the influence of Schumpeter and Redlich at the Harvard School of Business Administration. In this research context, too, the social origins of the business elite were investigated mainly during the decade immediately after the Second World War and particularly intensively in the USA. Since then, historical studies on the recruitment of the business elite have appeared only sporadically. It is only during the last few years that publications and projects have begun to build up again and even then mainly on the history of the German business elite.

Although the recruitment of major businessmen is regarded as an indicator for the degree of openness of industrial society and has, therefore, considerable potential for controversy, it has not in fact been the subject of intense historical debate. The main reason for this is that historical research on businessmen involves too many linguistic, geographical and professional barriers for scientific exchange. It certainly cannot be attributed to the fact that previous investigations have all reached identical conclusions and produced clear-cut interpretations. On this topic too, the various positions can be outlined most clearly if developments during the industrial revolution, in the broad sense of the term, are analysed first, followed by developments during the twentieth century. The research studies on these two periods are, however, very closely related to one another as will become clear.

Industrialisation

In the classic works of economic and social history one frequently comes across the theory that, during the industrial revolution, businessmen derived from all social classes and occupations. This thesis is usually linked with the sceptical assumption that afterwards, with the emergence of large-scale enterprises at the end of the nineteenth and the beginning of the twentieth centuries, the economic elite became increasingly exclusive. The theory of the industrial revolution as the epoch of the self-made man was formulated by a generation of social scientists who had themselves been eye-witnesses of the rapid economic concentration of the prewar period, above all in the USA and Germany, and of the economic crises of the interwar period, and who therefore viewed the industrial revolution in a very positive light. These ideas are based mainly on theoretical deductions or impressionistic observations which have not yet been subjected to examination by modern methods of quantification. They recur in the majority of economic history textbooks, even those published quite recently.

There are not many quantitative works which support this thesis, and those dealing with Europe are particularly scarce. A. Schröter, who examined the social origins of German industrialists in the engineering sector before 1850, who were still operating on the basis of very limited capital and expertise, came to the conclusion that only a third of them had fathers who were businessmen, while half of them had fathers who were peasants and, above all, artisans. There may also have been some whose fathers were skilled workers. In the British hosiery industry (which has been investigated by Charlotte Erickson in an excellent study), in 1871 almost half the industrialists had fathers who were self-employed artisans, small retailers, white-collar employees and workers. By the beginning of the twentieth century, recruitment to this entrepreneurial group was becoming more exclusive — entirely in accordance with the thesis of the golden age of the industrial revolution — and there were noticeably more businessmen whose fathers were themselves businessmen. According to a recent and very careful research survey by P.L. Payne, it is not improbable that the British businessmen of the nineteenth century came predominantly from the 'lower levels of the middle ranks' of British society and that, as a result of the emergence of large firms in the late nineteenth century in Britain, the opportunities for upward movement into top positions in business were reduced. Payne, however, places great emphasis on the lack of really reliable information.

In contrast, there is much more weighty evidence of a particularly open recruitment of businessmen during the industrial revolution for the USA. The only study which can confirm this for the businessmen of a whole country is that of C. Wright Mills on the USA. In an analysis based on the 'Dictionary of the American Biography' he shows that only a third of the American business elite born around 1800 had fathers who were businessmen, whereas almost half had fathers who were farmers, artisans and workers,and they were less likely than before to be university graduates. In the following generations there were increasingly more businessmen whose fathers were businessmen: 29 per cent of the 1790-1819 generation, but already 48 per cent of the 1850-79 generation. Mills's thesis of the opportunities for social ascent of the self-made man during the industrial revolution has recently been put forward by Herbert C. Gutman in a work which, significantly, like that of Schröter, deals with the engineering industry. In a local study of industrialists in the iron and engineering industry in Paterson (New Jersey), Gutman came to the conclusion that the typical industrialist in this sector was either a skilled worker who had moved to the town or had served an apprenticeship in one of the firms in Paterson. In Gutman's view, this demonstrates that there is some truth in the myth of the self-made man; he presumes that investigations of other new American cities would produce similar results.[2]

The majority of works on the social origins of businessmen during the industrial revolution reach different conclusions. Apart from Mills's study, there are a whole series of investigations of the business elite in the USA covering both the country as a whole as well as particular sectors of industry. The most important one is by Reinhard Bendix and Frank W. Howton, who analyse the development of the recruitment of the American business elite on the basis of the National Cyclopedia of American Biography and, at the same time, provide a very good review of research in the field. They come to the conclusion that the recruitment of the American business elite was by no means open during the industrial revolution. More than two-thirds had fathers who were large landowners or, above all, businessmen. The sons of landowners became fewer and those of businessmen more numerous in accordance with the change in the economic structure. Only about one in ten businessmen had a father who was a peasant; businessmen whose fathers were artisans or workers were even rarer (see Table 5.1). The

Table 5.1: The social origins of the business elite in the USA 1771-1920 (per cent)

| Father's occupation | Year of birth | | | | |
	1771-1800	1801-1830	1831-1860	1861-1890	1891-1920
Businessmen	40	52	66	70	69
Gentry farmers	25	11	3	3	5
Subtotal	65	63	69	73	74
Master craftsmen and small entrepreneurs	9	4	3	1	
Professionals	3	12	11	12	11
government officials[a]	4	7	3	3	3
White-collar workers incl. foremen	7	2	2	3	6
Subtotal	23	25	19	19	20
Farmers	12	11	10	6	4
Manual workers		2	1	2	3
Subtotal	12	13	11	8	7
Full total	100	100	100	100	100
Number in sample	125	89	360	380	143
Father's occupation recorded	91	56	225	281	106
Father's occupation not recorded	34	33	135	99	37
Proportion of sample without details of father's occupation	27	37	37	26	26

[a]Includes some school officials and army officers.
Source: R. Bendix & F.W. Howton, 'Social Mobility and the American Business Elite' in S.M. Lipset & R. Bendix (eds.), *Social Mobility in Industrial Society* (Berkeley, Los Angeles, 1963), p. 122.

high proportion of the business elite who had the favourable start in life provided by a privileged family — surprising in the land of the self-made man — remained remarkably stable during the nineteenth century and increased still further during and immediately after the industrial revolution. The education of the American business elite also shows that only very few of those from the lower, unskilled occupational groups (like the famous dishwashers) achieved top positions in business. The majority of the business elite was educated at high schools or business schools, if not at universities; only a tiny proportion of the American population in the nineteenth century possessed these educational advantages. Bendix and Howton, therefore, consider that the thesis of spectacular entrepreneurial careers being made during the industrial revolution, and of the reduction in these opportunities for upward movement after the industrial revolution, has been disproved – at any rate for the USA. In their opinion, the reason why their results diverged so markedly from those of Mills's study was, above all, because they used a different and more appropriate collection of biographical data.

Bendix and Howton's thesis has been confirmed by other studies. Frances W. Gregory and Irene D. Neu investigated the origins of American industrialists in the leading firms in what were in those days the three most important branches of industry – railways, textiles and steel – during the 1860s. They too came to the conclusion that the majority of American industrialists came from family backgrounds which were very favourable from the economic point of view: half of them came from entrepreneurial families and a quarter from those of big landowners. These industrialists had also reached a very high standard of education according to their survey: two thirds had attended high school or even college. Thus, Gregory and Neu also considered that a self-made man such as Carnegie was not typical of American industrialists. Investigations of particular business sectors during the 1870s have confirmed this impression. It may not be surprising that three-quarters of American bankers came from entrepreneurial families. One might also anticipate that three-quarters of the directors of American railway companies in this period which saw the beginnings of economic concentration came from the families of academics, civil servants and above all businessmen. Moreover, according to Gregory and Neu, half the American steel industrialists during the 1870s also came from entrepreneurial families and probably a considerable number from a big landowning or professional background, despite the fact that the introduction of the Bessemer process produced a phase of reorganisation in the American steel industry and one would, therefore, have anticipated a much larger proportion of outsiders. Finally, over half the industrialists in the American textile industry came from entrepreneurial families and probably a further number from favourable backgrounds within the upper and upper-middle strata. Stimulated by Gutman's thesis, John Ingham has recently investigated the American steel industry once more, but on the basis of more extensive material and over a longer period than in the case of Gregory and Neu. Ingham was primarily interested in the question of whether or not significant differences would emerge between individual American cities and, therefore, analysed six American cities separately (Philadelphia, Pittsburgh, Cleveland, Youngstown, Bethlehem and Wheeling). Ingham's study provided confirmation for the thesis that almost all the industrialists in the iron and steel industry came from privileged families, and that those who had moved up from the working class almost invariably represented a small minority. He suggested, however, that the opportunities for social ascent were much more favourable in cities which had been recently established and were mainly of medium size with a social structure which had not yet become consolidated, than in established cities such as Philadelphia or Pittsburgh (see Table 5.2).[3]

Few of the works on the European business elite during the industrial revolution support the classic thesis. Charlotte Erickson — to return to one of the best historical studies of the recruitment of industrialists in Europe — demonstrated that in the British steel industry, the second branch of industry which she investigated, in 1865 two-thirds of the industrialists themselves came from entrepreneurial families and that only one tenth came from the lower middle or working classes. As in the USA, this situation did not change despite the technological revolution involved in the Bessemer process. In her view, this can be explained, at least in part, in terms of the powerful role played by the family among British steel industrialists. She also shows that approximately half the industrialists in the steel industry came from the small section of the British population who had received secondary education. The top managers of the leading British railway companies between 1850 and 1922, investigated by Terence R. Gourvish, also came mainly from the upper and upper middle classes, above all from entrepreneurial families and the families of those with higher education. The majority of these had also attended grammar or public schools. Gourvish attributes this exclusive recruitment above all to the personnel policies of the railway companies who preferred managers with secondary education and a wealthy family background.[4]

As far as France is concerned, Maurice Lévy-Leboyer, in particular, has attempted to provide an initial overview of the trend of recruitment and qualifications of the French business elite since the industrial revolution. In his view, too, the French *patrons* during the nineteenth century were a relatively closed class. There are, however, as yet only a few quantitative surveys on the social origins of French businessmen during the industrial revolution; Lévy-Leboyer developed

Table 5.2: The social origins of American iron and steel industrialists 1874-1900 (per cent)

Father's occupation	Phila-delphia (1)	Pitts-burgh (2)	Cleve-land (3)	Youngs-town (4)	Bethle-hem (5)	Wheeling (6)
Manufacturers	60	59	40	46	39	51
Merchants	13	9	21	13	31	12
Bankers	5	2	7	0	0	0
Businessmen total	78	70	68	59	70	63
Professions	11	14	16	20	15	15
Workers	9	9	13	7	15	20
Farmers	2	6	2	14	0	2
Total	100	100	100	100	100	100
Number in sample	104	360	86	70	14	62

Source: J.N. Ingham, 'Rags to Riches Revisited: The Effect of City Size and Related Factors on the Recruitment of Business Leaders', *Journal of American History* (1976), p. 634. See also Ingham, *The Iron Barons. A Social Analysis of an American Urban Elite* (Westport, Conn., 1978).

his thesis indirectly on the basis of the longevity of French firms and the limited number of new firms established during the nineteenth century. In his view, the established entrepreneurial families and the heavily capitalised *marchand-fabricants* left little scope for outsiders in French industry. The point was confirmed by Theodore Zeldin, who analysed the view of industry as a career found in popular books on psychology and career guidance published in the nineteenth and early twentieth centuries. In his opinion, this literature made a decisive contribution to the low esteem in which industry was held as a career in France. Above all, in the nineteenth century, people were warned of the risks of going into industry and were advised to follow a more secure career in the civil service or the professions. Even in the early twentieth century, those who were upwardly mobile were only conceded genuine opportunities in the tertiary sector. The top positions in industry were regarded as virtually inaccessible because of the dominance of the family firms. Non-quantitive investigations focusing on particular industries, such as those by Bertrand Gille on the French iron industrialists, by Claude Fohlen and Jean Lambert Dansette on the French textile industrialists, and by G. Thuiller and again by Gille on the French bankers, also conclude that French businessmen during the industrial revolution were largely recruited from industry itself and that upwardly mobile people were rare.[5]

In the case of Germany, Wilhelm Stahl and the author of this research account have independently (and without knowledge of one another's work) utilised the articles on businessmen in the *Neue Deutsche Biographie*. Both surveys concluded that the recruitment of German industrialists during the industrial revolution was exclusive. In Germany, too, the majority of the business elite had fathers who were themselves businessmen, and only a small proportion came from the lower middle class and from peasants' and workers' families. Nor did this change after the industrial revolution (see Table 5.3). Several

Table 5.3: The social origins of the German business elite 1800-1965

Father's occupation	1800-1870 (%) (1)	1871-1914 (%) (2)	1918-1933 (%) (3)	1964 (%) (4)	1965 (%) (5)
High rank civil servants[a]	10	9	7	5	6
Professions	1	3	3	18	7
Big landowners	2	2	4	–	–
Businessmen	54	53	53	36	21
Artisans, retailers, publicans	24	20	16	5	15
Farmers	2	4	4	2	3
Middle rank civil servants	5	7	5	17	24
White-collar employees	1	2	7	3	13
Workers	0	0	1	5	5
Others	0	0	1	–	–
Total	100	100	100	100	100
Number in sample	235	297	232	118	537

[a]Includes officers, clergymen, university teachers, secondary school teachers.
Sources: Col. 1-2: H. Kaelble, 'Sozialer Aufstieg in Deutschland, 1850-1914', in *Vierteljahrschrift für Sozial- und Wirtschaftsgeschichte*, 60 (1973), p. 52; col. 3: H. Kaelble, 'Sozial Mobilität in Deutschland 1900-1960', in H. Kaelble (ed.), *Probleme der Modernisierung in Deutschland* (Opladen, 1978); col. 4: W. Zapf, 'Die Deutschen Manager' in W. Zapf (ed.), *Beiträge zur Analyse der deutschen Oberschicht* (München, 1965) p. 139 (board members of the fifty largest industrial undertakings in the Federal Republic); col. 5: H. Pross & K.W. Boetticher, *Manager des Kapitalismus* (Frankfurt, 1971), pp. 33, 43 (board members, directors and *Prokuristen* in thirteen large public companies in the Federal Republic).

regional investigations employing quantitative methods point in the same direction. Horst Beau studied the education of businessmen in the Rhineland and Westphalia between 1790 and 1870. He demonstrates that, as early as the 1830s, the great majority of businessmen had received secondary education, and a smaller but rapidly growing proportion, university education. The recent works on the distribution of opportunities at secondary schools, technical colleges and universities in the early nineteenth century, mentioned in the previous section, lead one to suppose that they referred mainly to sons from the upper middle class, more rarely from the lower middle class and not at all from the working class. A survey by W. Huschke on Thuringian businessmen between 1840 and 1880 leads one to conclude that nearly three-quarters of them came from the families of industrialists. As many as four-fifths of the Berlin business elite, whose social origins were investigated by the author of this study for the period between 1830 and 1870, had fathers who were businessmen. This particularly exclusive recruitment of the Berlin business elite can be explained by the remarkably high percentage of Jewish businessmen in the Berlin area. Owing to the restricted occupational opportunities of the Jewish minority before the industrial revolution, not only was the percentage of Jews particularly high among businessmen, but during the industrial revolution their management was also particularly family-orientated. Toni Pierenkemper has shown that during the period 1853-1913 the heavy industrialists in the Rhineland and Westphalia were also characterised by exclusive recruitment. A high proportion of industrialists came from the upper middle class and again had fathers who were industrialists; few came from artisan or peasant families, and only a very small proportion from working-class families. Nearly three-quarters of the industrialists had taken the *Abitur* and thus belonged to the 1-2 per cent of the German population who possessed this school-leaver's certificate, and again roughly three-quarters had been through higher education. A number of studies of businessmen which do not use quantification methods, and particularly those by Rolf Engelsing on Bremen, Wolfram Fischer on Baden and Wolfgang Zorn on Bavarian Swabia, and an international comparative investigation by the author of this study, are also unanimous in stressing the low number of those who were upwardly mobile among the business elite during the industrial revolution.[6]

German research has been particularly interested in the question of the initial occupations of those who later became businessmen. This aspect is also covered by the classic thesis that businessmen were recruited from a wide range of occupations. Even though it was quickly established that hardly a single member of the business elite had begun as a peasant, a worker, a subordinate official or as one of the numerous domestic servants, there still remained those numerous successful careers – much rarer in the twentieth century – made by artisans with small businesses, who seized a favourable business opportunity and

quickly rose to become big industrialists. The Berlin engineering industrialist, Borsig, and the steel magnate, Jacob Mayer, founder of the
Bochum Verein, are well-known examples. Three reservations must,
however, be made: first, scholars using more traditional research
methods which do not involve quantitative techniques are often too
easily impressed by spectacular examples wich are particularly well
documented, but rarely prove typical. In a research account which
relies more heavily on studies using quantitative methods, Jürgen Kocka
has pointed out that the majority of the more substantial and economically significant businessmen had originated as merchants and that a
spectacular rise from artisan to member of the business elite was certainly not the general rule.[7] Secondly, vertical mobility is easily overestimated if career mobility alone is investigated and family background is not taken into account as well. More detailed investigations of
the recruitment of businessmen during industrialisation have repeatedly
demonstrated (for spectacular careers as well) the great importance of
the family − for education, for migration to economically favourable
locations, for initial capital, for the establishment of commercial
contacts, even for the appointment to the top posts in rapidly expanding firms − during industrialisation. Thirdly, romanticised descriptions of the economic opportunities for upward mobility during the
industrial revolution frequently underestimated the role of investment
capital as a barrier to mobility. The growing application of technology
and the increase in the size of firms progressively required large
amounts of investment capital which only a small proportion of the
population could raise, while conversely the banking system was still
in the process of development. At the same time, managerial careers −
the way to become a businessman without capital − were still rare
during the industrial revolution and, therefore,offered no real alternative for entrepreneurial talent lacking capital.

The Twentieth Century

The more recent quantitative research on the origins of businessmen
not only makes the more open recruitment of the business elite during
the industrial revolution appear rather improbable, it also does not
always accept the sceptical assumption of the increasing social exclusiveness of the entrepreneurial class after the industrial revolution.
There are, however, important works which do document the latter
assumption. Thus. T.W. Acheson has demonstrated that, between 1880
and 1910, among Canadian businessmen, upwardly mobile individuals
from the lower class became markedly less numerous and, around 1910,

almost all the top businessmen had fathers who were themselves businessmen or university graduates. He sees the decisive reason for this in the trend for privately-owned companies to be transformed into joint stock companies, in which an entrepreneurial career clearly required a higher level of education and in which the sons of businessmen lost some of their initial advantages, whereas men from the upper and upper middle classes were able to secure a more dominant position than they had had in the days of the private company. However, in Canada around 1880, access to top positions in industry appears to have been more open than in Europe and — if one makes a comparison with the survey by Bendix and Howton — than in the USA as well. In his essay, which has already been referred to, C. Wright Mills demonstrates that in the USA there was a marked increase in the number of businessmen whose fathers were businessmen during the course of the twentieth century. There was, however, only a marginal increase in the number of industrialists from the upper and upper middle classes. It remains, therefore, unclear whether or not there really were more businessmen who came from economically privileged families in the twentieth century. In the case of Great Britain, Payne assumed — as has already been mentioned — that the growing economic concentration since the end of the nineteenth century was associated with an increasingly exclusive recruitment of businessmen. Finally, in what is hitherto the only comprehensive survey of post-war Europe, M.M. Postan stresses not only the disproportionately high level of recruitment of businessmen from the upper and upper middle classes, which is not disputed by anyone; in his view, there are also one or two indications to suggest that this type of recruitment became more frequent in the twentieth century and that businessmen from working-class families became less numerous. He explained this tendency towards an exacerbation of economic inequality of opportunity in terms of the higher educational standards required for businessmen, with an academic education increasingly becoming a prerequisite for an entrepreneurial career.[8] Postan's argument, which he puts forward very tentatively, is, however, based only on the observation of sociological studies to the effect that the older British businessmen have tended to be upwardly mobile more frequently than the younger ones. This could be explained, however, by the fact that the upwardly mobile businessmen only secured top positions later in life than did the offspring of economically privileged families. At any rate, Postan's conclusions have not been confirmed by any British sociologists.

The majority of studies on the social origins of the business elite in the twentieth century point in another direction. In their book, which has already been referred to, Bendix and Howton, apart from their own study, reviewed the studies which have appeared on the American business elite and which are particularly numerous and thorough for the period of the twentieth century: that of Mabel Newcomer on the top managers of the approximately two hundred largest industrial and transport companies in the years 1893, 1923, and 1948; the study by Suzanne Keller of the managers of the largest concerns, including the banks, in the years 1870, 1900-10 and 1950; the survey by W.Lloyd Warner and James C. Abegglen, who investigated some 8,300 American businessmen in 1952 and compared their results with a similar survey of 1928. The main thesis of Bendix's and Howton's contribution is that all these studies show, in contrast to that of Mills, that while the proportion of businessmen from economically privileged families was high, it did not increase during the twentieth century but remained stable, and that the opportunities for social ascent from the impoverished lower social strata did not decrease. Bendix and Howton even see indications that during the twentieth century the opportunities for talented businessmen, who did not belong to the rich, Anglo-Saxon, protestant families born in the USA, may have improved somewhat. They believe, however, that during this period as well, family connections continued to have considerable importance for entrepreneurial careers. The studies by Keller and Newcomer, however, suggest a noticeable increase in entrepreneurial careers which were 'bureaucratic' in character and independent of family connections, and thus a slight reduction in the significance of social origins. Mabel Newcomer continued her study with a further survey in 1964. Her new results do not support the thesis of the growing exclusivity of top managers either; she even notes a slight increase in the number of executives from the families of non-supervisory employees and workers. Finally, James Soltow's work on the industrialists who founded the metal and engineering industries in New England between 1890 and 1952 does not support the thesis of the growing exclusiveness of entrepreneurial recruitment. Although he has not investigated family origins or dealt with the historical shifts in entrepreneurial recruitment, nevertheless his results show that, even during the twentieth century, a relatively large proportion of industrialists (31 per cent) began as skilled workers and the majority of them had only had elementary education. The great advantage of Soltow's study is that it does not — like almost all the contributions referred to — deal with the business elite but above all with medium-sized and small-scale industrialists and demon-

Table 5.4: The social origins of British managers at the time of their appointment 1925-55 (per cent)

Father's occupation	pre-1925 (1)	1925-29 (2)	1930-34 (3)	1935-39 (4)	1940-44 (5)	1945-49 (6)	1950-55 (7)
Professional and higher administration	28	29	23	21	12	17	22
Managerial and executive	12	22	19	18	10	16	17
Higher inspection and supervisory	4	7	10	16	7	9	13
Lower inspection and supervisory	20	24	28	17	32	20	21
Skilled manual	12	12	15	24	21	28	22
Semi-skilled manual	4	2	5	5	15	5	6
Unskilled manual	0	2	0	0	3	4	0
Total	100	100	100	100	100	100	100
Number in sample	25	41	79	83	61	181	181

Source: Estimated according to R.V. Clements, *Managers* (London, 1955), p. 186.

strates that recruitment into this stratum was relatively open during the twentieth century.[9]

The majority of the few historical works on the European business elite during the twentieth century also come to the conclusion that the recruitment of top businessmen remained unaltered or even became somewhat more open. There are, however, differing views on the extent of and the reasons for this development. In 1958, R.V. Clements investigated the development of the social origins of British managers. His results show neither a trend towards exclusiveness nor towards openness within the British entrepreneurial class (see Table 5.4). Philip Stanworth and Anthony Giddens, who analysed the recruitment of the chairmen of the fifty largest British companies between 1905 and 1971, support this thesis. Businessmen from the middle class and from the exclusive public schools retained their high proportion; and while the number of careers based on family connections declined, they still remained frequent. Stanworth and Giddens regard it as conceivable that the educational reforms of 1944 may have produced improved opportunities for upward movement in the business world (outside this small group of top businessmen) via the more socially accessible grammar schools. C. Erickson adopts a rather more optimistic position in her study, referred to above. She demonstrates that, after the First World War, the British steel magnates tended to come less frequently from the families of businessmen, big landowners and professional people. Their percentage declined from 82 per cent to 62 per cent. Industrialists from the lower middle class and from white-collar families became much more numerous (an increase from 2 per cent to 13 per cent) (see Table 5.5). The recruitment of British textile industrialists also became more open during the twentieth century, a period when a number of new firms were established. In the interwar years, the proportion of industrialists who had fathers who were businessmen declined sharply (from 54 per cent to 39 per cent), whereas industrialists from white-collar and blue-collar families became much more numerous (an increase from 14-39 per cent). In the case of both industries, Erickson regarded the decline in the number of privately-owned concerns and the growth of joint stock companies as the main reason for this development: the initial advantages possessed by the sons of industrialists, namely the possession of capital or the inheritance of a firm, were no longer such a decisive factor. Erickson does not, however, believe that this is the sole reason why the proportion of the sons of white-collar and blue-collar workers who had secured senior posts in the firms of a particular branch of industry increased. She considers an

Table 5.5: The social origins of British steel industrialists at the beginning of their careers 1865-1953 (per cent)

Father's occupation	1865	1875-1895	1905-1925	1935-1947	1953
Partner, owner, director same industry	28	31	36	28	21
Partner, owner, director other industry	19	15	15	8	8
Merchant or banker	13	8	4	6	5
Businessmen total	60	54	55	42	34
Landowner, farmer	13	13	7	10	7
Professional man	14	15	19	23	15
Senior manager or agent	2	4	6	5	6
Social Class I total	89	86	87	80	62
Retail tradesman	3	3	2	3	2
Clerk, foreman, salesman or book-keeper	2	4	4	7	13
Independent craftsman	2	4	3	1	5
Social Class II total	7	11	9	11	20
Skilled worker (employee)	3	1	2	8	14
Unskilled or semi-skilled worker	1	2	2	1	4
Social Class III and IV combined	4	3	4	9	18
Total	100	100	100	100	100
Number in sample	63	151	178	146	138
No information	7	14	9	8	1

Source: C. Erickson, *British Industrialists: Steel and Hosiery 1850-1950* (Cambridge, 1959), p. 12.

important factor to have been the change which took place in the boards of directors, which, after the 1930s, became more powerful in terms of making the major decisions and whose members were selected less and less on the basis of their social prestige and recruited more from the active executives who were more often upwardly mobile. Finally, Harold Perkin dealt with the chairmen of the two hundred largest private companies between 1880 and 1970. His results also show a very large proportion of the business elite coming from economically privileged families and, as he stresses, the continuing inequality of access to top posts in business. At the same time, however, recruitment became slightly less exclusive. In the first place, within the upper middle class the proportion of chairmen whose fathers were businessmen fell sharply, whereas the proportion of chairmen from professional families rose steeply. In addition, the chairmen came somewhat less frequently from the upper middle class and rather more frequently from the lower middle class. As with the other investigations, however, one gains the impression that the opportunities for access to top posts in business did not change for men from the working class (see Table 5.6). All in all, Perkin's investigation provides the clearest evidence for the thesis of the slight reduction in the exclusiveness of entrepreneurial recruitment in Great Britain.[10]

Table 5.6: The social origins of British business leaders 1880-1970 (per cent)

Father's occupation	1900-19	1920-39	1940-59	1960-70
Land	10.6	4.4	4.5	4.9
Business	59.6	54.6	51.5	46.3
Higher Professional	7.3	14.1	13.4	17.3
Upper middle	77.5	73.1	69.4	68.5
Farmer	2.6	2.0	0.5	1.2
Small Business	8.6	13.2	16.3	12.3
Lower Professional	4.0	5.4	6.9	8.0
Lower middle	15.2	20.6	23.7	21.5
Non-manual	2.6	3.9	3.0	4.9
Skilled manual	3.3	2.4	3.5	3.7
Semi- and Unskilled	1.3	–	0.5	1.2
Total	100.0	100.0	100.0	100.0
Number known	165	213	202	162

Source: H. Perkin, 'The Recruitment of Elites in British Society since 1880', *Journal of Social History* (Winter, 1980), Table 3.2 (without 1880-1899 since the sample is very small).

In the case of France, there have hitherto been no quantitative investigations of the historical development of the social origins of businessmen in the twentieth century. Maurice Lévy-Leboyer attempted to develop an initial thesis on the basis of some indications. In his view, the secular phase of prosperity which began around 1890 and the increased demand for technically and scientifically-educated businessmen may have led to a more socially open recruitment of the business elite. The change in the social origins of the pupils of the *grandes écoles*, the most important educational institutions for French businessmen, referred to above, appears to him an important indication of this. He emphasises, however, that the change in entrepreneurial recruitment was dependent on economic growth and that during the Great Depression the opportunities for ascent into entrepreneurial positions once more tended to be restricted.[11]

There are a number of studies of the German business elite in the twentieth century with, however, very varying emphases, and which unfortunately do not cover the particularly interesting period of the Third Reich and the postwar years, which were characterised by the most extensive circulation of elites. For both these reasons one can only make general assertions about broad trends. As with the case of British industrialists, the recruitment of major industrialists in Germany appears to have become somewhat more open during the twentieth century. There were noticeably fewer sons of businessmen; and there were far more industrialists whose fathers were white-collar employees, particularly middle-ranking civil servants (see Table 5.3). Here too, apart from the change in the structure of employment, two reasons in particular were decisive. In the first place, as a result of the decline in the number of private entrepreneurs and the increasing separation of the ownership of capital from its control, the opportunities for the sons of industrialists were considerably reduced while the chances for the sons of high-ranking civil servants and professional men to move into top positions in the business world were correspondingly increased. Secondly, after a time, the change in the distribution of opportunities in the universities of the Second Reich, referred to in the previous chapter, also began to have an effect. The increasing opportunities for academic education which became open to the children of middle-level civil servants in the Second Reich ensured that their chances of ascent improved in those entrepreneurial careers which, even before the First World War, had become subject to academic qualifications. In Germany, too, the professionalisation of the entrepreneurial career and the separation of the control of capital from its ownership had the effect of opening up the recruitment of industrialists to some extent; but the children of subordinate white-collar employees and – to an even greater extent than in the USA or in Britain – of workers continued to remain barred.[12]

All in all, postwar research has substantially revised the classic thesis that during the industrial revolution the business elite came from every occupational group and every social class, whereas after the industrial revolution, with the creation of big firms, recruitment became increasingly exclusive. Nowadays, we see the trend rather differently: the majority of works on the social origins of the business elite during the industrial revolution suggest that recruitment was extremely exclusive. In some branches of industry such as engineering and parts of the early textile industry, in which a rapid expansion of the plant was feasible with a relatively small initial outlay of capital, and in which the establishment and the expansion of firms required above all technical expertise, access to an entrepreneurial career in the early nineteenth century was undoubtedly remarkably open. Here one can find examples of men who were sons of artisans, workers and peasants, becoming industrialists. In other sectors of business, which were at least as growth-orientated, such as the steel industry, railways, mining and banking, because of the big requirement of capital the recruitment of businessmen was extremely exclusive even during the industrial revolution. In the course of the industrial revolution this kind of recruitment was much more typical for the business elite in general and can be explained in part by the fact that the majority of enterprises were family firms and were inherited; also on the basis of the great importance of the family in early industrial society, which was also true for those founding companies, and in terms of the personnel policies of firms and of traditional barriers to occupational mobility. With the rise of modern large-scale corporations recruitment did not become more exclusive. In the USA it appears to have remained unchanged. In those European cases where it has been investigated so far, some results suggest a small relative increase in businessmen from middle-level white-collar and civil service families, and in rare instances even from the working class. Three developments in particular are seen as decisive for this: first, the major increase in joint stock companies, and the separation of the control of capital from its ownership associated with it, markedly reduced the initial advantages of the sons of businessmen. Managerial careers which were not so heavily dependent on social origins improved the chances of the sons of high-level civil servants and professional men in particular. Secondly, the professionalisation of the entrepreneurial career and its subjection to academic qualifications ensured that the changes in the equality of opportunity at secondary schools and universities also made themselves apparent in the social origins of the business elite. Slight improvements in equality of opportunity in the educational field could lead to a somewhat more open recruitment of the business elite. However, this point is particularly controversial. Other authors emphasise that with the introduction of academic qualifications entrepreneurial careers were influenced more than before by the prerequisite of an academic education, with the result that previous opportunities for ascent were blocked off. Thirdly, changes in personnel policy concerning the appointment to top positions must have had an impact on the social origins of the business elite. Hitherto, however, this aspect has been only rarely and rather tentatively investigated and could prove equally controversial. All these studies emphasise that during the twentieth century the business elite has been drawn to a disproportionate extent from economically privileged families, and upwardly mobile individuals from non-supervisory civil service, white-collar and above all blue-collar families are heavily underrepresented. At the same time, the majority of authors underline the growing importance of education for entrepreneurial careers and, associated with this, the increasing possibilities for a policy geared towards equality of opportunity. Moreover, some rightly emphasise that the move away from the classic thesis on the recruitment of the business elite does not in itself permit an overall assessment of the position of that elite in twentieth century society, since nothing has yet been said about their economic power, their social privileges, their management qualities or their political behaviour. As far as the topic of social mobility is concerned, however, the historical research on the business elite which has been carried out over the past thirty years undoubtedly represents a watershed.

Postwar research has neglected three important aspects: first, for technical reasons it has hitherto restricted itself to a few hundred top businessmen. Almost nothing is known about the social origins of small and medium-scale businessmen or about their historical development. Undoubtedly, managerial careers are less frequent among this group and it is quite possible that the recruitment of these businessmen developed very differently. Secondly, it is not entirely clear whether the somewhat more open recruitment of the business elite during the twentieth century represents a structurally determined trend or only a passing consequence of the secular phase of economic prosperity after the Second World War. More investigations are necessary on this point and, in particular, ones spaced closer together in time. Thirdly, and finally, too little attention has been paid to the reasons for the change in the recruitment patterns of top businessmen. It has still not been properly explained what role was played by changes in the career assistance given by the family, by changes in the educational system, and by changes in the practice of the selection and promotion of businessmen. This last issue is particularly crucial for a society which is concerned about equality of opportunity and is dependent on the full utilisation of scarce talent.

The Political Elite

The only other elite group which has been intensively investigated in terms of the long-term change in its social origins is the political elite, since it is often regarded as a kind of barometer for the trend in the distribution of opportunities in the parliamentary democracies of developed countries. Most of these historical studies are concerned with Western Europe and use a remarkably similar approach, which is not simply the result of a common intellectual outlook but – as will become clear in the following pages – is also prompted by similar historical developments and current problems which are shared by West European countries. Two arguments in particular, are repeatedly advanced and examined empirically: firstly, Robert Michels's iron law of oligarchy with which he wished to prove that in mass political organisations there is an inexorable tendency for a gap to develop between the mass membership and the cadre of functionaries and that, through the nature of their recruitment, the functionaries increasingly separate themselves off from the membership. Secondly, Max Weber's thesis of the gradual replacement of the honorary politician by the professional politician. The honorary politician normally regards politics as a sideline; his success depends less on his programme than on his personality; he is seldom closely linked to stable political organisations, indeed he exists in periods of still unstable and unbureaucratic political organisations, and he – the decisive factor as far as this study is concerned – usually comes from the upper social stratum. The professional politician, however, is entirely dependent on politics for his livelihood; he moves up into the political elite through a career linked to stable political organisations and may come from any social stratum or class. These two historical theses, which provide very different descriptions of the recruitment of the political elite, have become so much a part of the discussion on political elites that they are frequently put forward without specific reference to Michels and Weber. Both arguments have been important starting points for historical research. But, although this research has been continuing since the interwar years, historians have been rare participants and, for a long time, it was carried out by a very small group of sociologists and political scientists. Only recently have there been signs of a wider interest in the subject – at any rate in Britain.[13]

The change in the recruitment into top political positions has been particularly thoroughly investigated in Great Britain. In a whole series of publications on the history of the British political elite in the nineteenth and twentieth centuries, W. L. Guttsman has suggested that two particular developments have taken place in elite recruitment. First, he emphasises the more open access to the political elite in Great Britain (i.e. membership of Parliament and of the Cabinet) in the last decades of the nineteenth and the first decades of the twentieth centuries. Among the Conservative and Liberal Members of Parliament and of the government, the proportion of the bourgeoisie and, to a lesser extent, of the professions rose sharply. At the same time, with the rise of the Labour Party, members of the working class increased noticeably. Guttsman sees in this transformation of the social background of the British political elite not only a direct consequence of the phased introduction of universal suffrage between 1867 and 1918, but, above all, the result of the emergence of tightly organised parties, also at local level, and the development of a class-orientated workers' party – the Labour Party. Secondly, in Guttsman's view, during the twentieth century, and particularly in the Labour Party, there was a trend towards oligarchy, towards a growing discrepancy between the social background of the party politicians and the social background of the electoral base. He shows that workers became increasingly rare among Labour MPs and members of the Cabinet, particularly after the Second World War; at the same time, the proportion of university graduates increased and, in this way, the social background of labour politicians became increasingly similar to that of the Conservative Party. The main reasons for this *embourgeoisement* of the Labour Party and for the convergence of the social backgrounds of the Labour and Conservative parties are, in his opinion, first, the fact that Labour politicians were less frequently career trade unionists by origin. Particular trade unions were less and less in a position to control individual constituencies and, as a consequence, lost influence on the selection of Labour Party candidates. Secondly, in Guttsman's view, the appeal of the Labour Party in working-class constituencies was based less and less on social solidarity and increasingly on 'rational' political goals. As a result, it became less important from what social class the Labour Party MPs came. In a study published in 1972, Peter Pulzer also considered that recruitment to the British elite had tended to become more and more determined by academic qualifications in the post-war period and, in this respect, there was a growing similarity between the social origins and educational background of politicians in the two most important British parties. He attributed this change less to the declining influence of the trade unions on the selection of Labour Party candidates and more to the general professionalisation of the political elite and to the expansion of secondary and higher education. R.W. Johnson, who investigated the recruitment of the British elite between 1955 and 1972, fully supported the observations of Guttsman and Pulzer, but suggested a rather different explanation for the *embourgeoisement* of the Labour Party. In the first place, in his opinion, the Labour Party could, in competition with the Conservatives, demonstrate its competence to govern,

Table 5.7: The social origins of British Labour Party ministers 1900-70 (per cent)

Father's occupation	1900-1919	1920-1939	1940-1959	1960-1970
Land	–	4.0	5.9	2.9
Business	–	12.0	2.9	–
Higher Professional	–	12.0	20.6	25.7
Upper middle	–	28.0	28.4	28.6
Farmer	–	8.0	2.9	–
Small Business	25.0	12.0	11.8	17.1
Lower Professional	–	16.0	14.7	14.3
Lower middle	25.0	36.0	29.4	31.4
Non-manual	25.0	8.0	5.9	5.7
Skilled manual	25.0	24.0	35.3	31.4
Semi- and Unskilled	–	4.0	–	2.9
Total	100.0	100.0	100.0	100.0
Number known	4	25	34	35

Source: Perkin, 'The Recruitment of Elites', Table 1.1

Table 5.8: The social origins of British Conservative Party ministers 1880-1970 (per cent)

Father's occupation	1880-1899	1900-1919	1920-1939	1940-1959	1960-1970
Land	60.0	50.0	40.7	26.6	14.6
Business	11.4	7.7	20.3	20.3	22.0
Higher Professional	17.1	15.4	15.3	24.1	26.8
Upper middle	88.5	73.1	76.3	71.0	63.4
Farmer	0.0	–	1.7	1.3	–
Small business	2.9	3.8	1.7	12.7	17.1
Lower Professional	8.6	21.2	–	10.1	17.1
Lower middle	11.5	25.0	3.4	24.1	34.2
Non-manual	–	–	20.3	3.8	2.4
Skilled manual	–	1.9	–	1.3	–
Semi- and Unskilled	–	–	–	–	–
Total	100.0	100.0	100.0	100.0	100.0
Number known	35	52	59	79	41

Source: Perkin, 'The Recruitment of Elites', Table 1.3.

among other ways, by securing politicians with high educational qualifications. It was thus compelled to adopt as parliamentary candidates and as Cabinet members a growing number of university graduates. Secondly, university graduates joined the Labour Party in greater numbers than before because, after the Second World War, it formed the government more frequently and thus became a more attractive career prospect. Johnson also appears to have some doubts about the way in which the Labour Party had become more middle class and about its increasing similarity to the Conservative Party. At least a proportion of the graduates among Labour politicians were, in his opinion, middle class only in their occupational background and had often ascended from the lower middle or working class and still remained committed to the class from which they came. In addition, he sees signs of the emergence of political families in the Labour Party and gives some examples of Labour politicians whose fathers were Labour politicians and who, therefore, no longer came from the working class, but in terms of their social origins could only be considered middle class in a formal sense. It is particularly clear from his work that it is not sufficient to discuss the thesis of the *embourgeoisement* of the Labour Party simply by analysing the historical changes in the original careers and education of the political elite. Victor J. Hanby, who analysed the social origins and careers of the executive committee of the Labour Party between 1900 and 1970, noted in relation to this body the same remarkable decline in the number of workers and increase in university graduates as had occurred among Labour MPs and explained this change also in terms of the requirements of an expanding governing party and of the flood of graduates into a party of government. Hanby is particularly aware of the danger that this process will alienate the Labour Party from its working-class voters and fears that the fact of workers becoming Labour politicians will soon become just as much a political myth as that of dishwashers becoming big industrialists. The study of the British elite between 1880 and 1970 by Harold Perkin, already referred to, confirms the thesis of Guttsman concerning the Conservative Party, but arrives at rather different results as far as the Labour Party is concerned, above all because, apart from educational background, Perkin only analysed the father's occupation and not the original occupation. According to his results, even in the interwar period, a quarter of the Labour ministers had attended the exclusive public schools and almost half had been to university. Moreover, at that time, a quarter of the Labour ministers came from the upper middle class and only a third from the working class. The importance of Perkin's results lies in the fact that, since then, this educational and social background has only altered slightly if at all. Ministers without higher education only decreased slightly from 46 per cent to 34 per cent, ministers from working-class families did not become less numerous but even increased slightly. If one examines family background, the process of *embourgeoisement* in the Labour Party appears, according to Perkin's data, to have already been completed by the time the party came to power and since then to have remained static. There remained considerable differences between the family backgrounds of the Conservative and Labour party leaderships.[14]

In the case of France, historical change in the recruitment of the political elite has been analysed less frequently but the issues have been more controversial. Studies of the revolutionary era using quantitative methods appear to have been carried out only recently: Guy Chauss-inand-Nogaret, Louis Bergeron and Robert Forster are at the moment investigating *notables* around 1800 on the basis of the electoral colleges of the Paris National Assembly and of the local administration. They are not really dealing with top political positions but with hundreds of thousands of political offices. Initial results for five *départements* which appear representative, both for agrarian as well as early indus-trial France, show how strongly the Napoleonic *notables* corresponded to the type of the honorary politician. The great majority of the *notables* were merchants, members of the professions, or came from the landowning class, and, as a result, possessed high social prestige, functional authority and economic power. In addition, wealth, partic-ularly in the form of landed property, was crucial for membership of the *notables*. All these are criteria which typically legitimise political domination in a society of honorary politicians. It was, however, char-acteristic for Napoleonic *notables* that, as a consequence of the French Revolution — as the authors emphasise — there was, for a predomin-antly agrarian country, a relatively small proportion of agrarian prop-erty owners. Moreover, in comparison to Germany, it is noticeable that very few *notables* came from the higher civil service.

The effects of the Revolution of 1830 on the political elite in France have also been studied more frequently in recent years. The discussion revolves mainly round the question of whether the Revolu-tion brought the bourgeoisie to power. Patrice Higonnet was the first to carry out a quantitative investigation of the social composition of the Chamber of Deputies immediately before and after 1830 and came to the conclusion that after 1830 the deputies were younger, less affluent, and more bourgeois than before. In Higonnet's view, there-fore, one can indeed speak of a growth in power of the bourgeois, albeit little used, provided one takes the bourgeois to mean not only indus-trialists, whose proportion among the deputies did not change, but above all non-aristocratic groups. David H. Pinkney attacked this thesis with the argument that the social background of the French Cabinet and of the Chamber of Deputies changed only slightly between 1829 and 1831 and that there is nothing to indicate that the *grande bourge-oisie*, which in his eyes is the section that mattered, gained in political power. Pinkney does not deny that a far-reaching change in the political elite took place, but sees it mainly in the shape of the return of the Napoleonic political elite, a point which has also been made by Higonnet. T.D. Beck, who investigated the social background of the Chamber of Deputies over the long term, confirms Higonnet's thesis. He too shows that, with the revolution of 1830, the number of landowners and nobles clearly decreased, whereas the bourgeoisie, among them solicitors and pro-government industrialists, clearly increased and, therefore, the July Monarchy represented an increase in power for the French bourgeoisie. All the participants in this discussion, however, see clearly that recruitment studies are of of only limited value as evidence for the question of political power and that they cannot provide a sub-stitute for a thorough analysis of the processes of political decision-making.

For a long time Mattei Dogan was the only scholar working on the social origins of the French political elite in the late nineteenth and twentieth centuries. In a series of articles he put forward the view that the social origins of the members of the French Parliament and French government between 1871 and the present day were undergoing a process of democratisation. While deputies and Cabinet ministers from the aristocracy and the *haute bourgeoisie* became less numerous, the proportion of politicians from the *petite bourgeoisie* and working class increased. Simultaneously, politicians with a university degree became rarer. Dogan's articles usually limited themselves to a description of this change and left open the reasons for it. In his article, published in 1973, Jean Charlot attacked this thesis. He demonstrated that since the Third Republic the proportion of workers among French deputies has not increased, that during the last few years it has even decreased, not only in the Socialist Party but in the Communist Party as well, that at the same time deputies with university degrees have increased rapidly and that, therefore, the same process could be observed occurring in France as in Great Britain. This process of the *embourgeoisement* of the Left, to which the majority of politicians from the working class belonged, was, in Charlot's view, triggered off by two causes: first, there was inexorable pressure on the mass parties of the Left to build up political cadres capable of governing. In comparison with that, the need to reflect the social background of the voters of the Left i.e. in-cluding the working class, in the governing bodies of the left-wing parties became less important. Secondly, through the expansion of secondary education in France it became increasingly feasible to recruit graduates into the governing bodies of both parties. Charlot points out that in the French parliament there is a growing number of professional politicians whose careers usually last for many years, gradually leading from local elected offices into parliament, and who are closely linked to party organisations. He sees in this a stabilising factor for the trend in recruitment of the political elite in France and for the trend towards the *embourgeoisement* of the Left. Charlot considers discontinuities in the French political elite, such as occurred during the Nazi occupation and the Fifth Republic, to be much less significant than does Dogan.[15]

The transition from honorary politician to professional politician in the last decades of the nineteenth century and the first decades of the twentieth century, and the tendency for the political elite to become an oligarchy in the postwar period appear to be European phenomena which can be observed in Germany as well. Here, however, because of the change in the political system, because of the late introduction of parliamentary government in 1918, because of the establishment of the Nazi elite in 1933, and because of the emergence of the Federal Republic between 1945 and 1949, the processes either occurred precipitately or overlapped and were concealed. Postwar research on the history of the political elite in Germany before 1945 and in the Federal Republic justifiably dealt primarily with the effects of this change of system, with the real significance of the Revolution of 1918, with the reasons for the establishment of the Nazi elite, and with the links between the political elite of the early Federal Republic and not only Weimar but also the Nazi period. This research was concerned more with the contribution of the political elites in Germany to the political catastrophes of the first half of the century and rightly less with the question of the avenues of access to the political elite. Several studies, however, show changes in the social background of the political elite occurring before 1918 and after 1945 similar to those in France and Britain. In a suggestive article strongly influenced by Max Weber, James Sheehan shows that Imperial Germany represents a decisive phase in the development of the political elite in Germany during which the transition from honorary politician to professional politician occurred and recruitment to the political elite became socially more open. The honorary politicians who, according to Sheehan, were mostly members of the German upper class, i.e. landowners, top civil servants, university professors or industrialists, who regarded politics as a hobby not as a profession, and whose political legitimacy lay above all in the social prestige of their profession, became much less numerous even in the Reichstag of the Second Reich. The effects of universal suffrage and of the rapidly increasing, even if frequently still passive, political mobilisation at elections and through pressure-group activity, the development of stable party organisations, of interest groups and trade unions, the emergence of the political form of the labour movement – all produced a new type of politician. His career was closely linked with political organisations; his success was not dependent on his original occupation but on his political activity and performance; he was to a much greater extent upwardly mobile from the lower middle and working classes and from occupational groups such as writers or white-collar employees. This removal of barriers to upward mobility in politics was of course limited above all by the fact that the Reichstag in the Second Reich had no influence on the appointment of the members of the government. The social background of the German Cabinet did not change rapidly until the introduction of parliamentary democracy in 1918 – as Knight has shown (see Table 5.9). Only then did it adapt itself to the social background of the deputies.[16]

Table 5.9: The social origins of the German political elite 1890-1933 (per cent)

Father's occupation	Imperial Germany (1890-1918)	Weimar Republic (1918-33)	NS-Period* (1933-45)
Business	10.4	18.9	18.2
Civil service	23.6	4.9	12.1
Landowners	18.4	6.6	12.1
Military	9.1	4.9	12.1
Law	18.4	1.6	–
Labour	1.3	11.5	3.0
Education	–	3.3	6.1
Medicine	1.3	3.3	3.0
Banking/insurance	4.0	0.8	–
Journalists, writers	2.6	0.8	–
Party leader	2.6	–	–
Ecclesiastical	2.6	–	–
Clerical, sales	–	1.6	–
Farming	–	0.8	3.0
No information	24.9	44.2	24.2
Nobility	64.5	11.5	27.3
Middle class	35.5	77.8	69.7
Working class	–	10.7	3.0

*Cabinet members.
Source: M. Knight, *The German Executive 1890-1933* (Stanford, 1955). p. 45 (upper part of the table), p. 33 (lower part of the table). The upper part of the table does not add up to 100.

The recruitment of the political elite after 1918 has been frequently investigated. The Nazi elite, in particular, has been analysed in various ways. David Lerner, who – on the basis of the *Führerlexikon* of 1934 – investigated the social origins, education and career of the Nazi elite as a whole, of the Nazi propagandists, of the top people in the Party organisation and in the military and the police, saw in the Nazi seizure of power above all the establishment of marginal men, a rise of the 'plebeians' from the lower social strata. Lerner, however, did not make any comparisons with earlier or later political systems in Germany. However, Maxwell E. Knight, who examined the social origins, educational background and careers of Cabinet ministers during the latter part of the Second Reich, the Weimar Republic and the Nazi era, considered the early Weimar Republic as the epoch which provided the most favourable opportunities for ascent into the political elite, since in those days a particularly large number of workers became ministers via the trade unions and the Social Democratic Party. According to Knight, fewer members of the Nazi Cabinet only had elementary education and had originally had working-class occupations, and more came from the aristocracy than in the Weimar Republic (see Table 5.9). The assessments made in later publications have also remained varied. David Schoenbaum, who dealt in a more comprehensive way with the opportunities for upward mobility into the upper and upper middle classes during the Nazi period, emphasised the favourable opportunities for social ascent in this regime. In his study of the elites in Germany and the Federal Republic between 1919 and 1955 Wolfgang Zapf defined two developments: on the one hand, the professionalisation of the political elite which, as in other European countries, over the long term led to a growing proportion of university graduates and to a declining proportion of workers among the top politicians; on the other hand, the effects of the change in the political system on the recruitment of the political elite. The seizure of power by the Nazi Party did lead to a far-reaching substitution of the political elite, to a different distribution of power between the top political positions, to greater opportunities for outsiders and thus initially to a more vigorous circulation of the top political positions. After the seizure of power, however, the circulation within the political elite was much less than in the Weimar Republic. Moreover, Zapf's figures show, as does Knight's study, that access to the political elite in the Nazi era was not more open than in the Weimar Republic. Politicians from the lower middle class not only became more numerous but also largely excluded those from the lower class. (see Table 5.10). The opportunities for upward movement into the political elite which had existed for workers during the Weimar Republic via trade unions, the workers' parties, and the Centre Party, were destroyed by the Nazi government. The proportion of university graduates was not lower during the Nazi era because the proportion of those from elementary schools was higher, but because more Nazi politicians were graduates of technical colleges or had not completed their studies.[17]

Table 5.10:The social origins of the German and West German political elite* 1925-55 (per cent)

Father's social class	1925	1940	1955
Mobility	7	7	6
Upper middle class	36	28	34
Lower middle class	28	46	34
	12	4	14
No data	17	16	11
Total	100	100	100
Number in sample	69	76	64

*Members of Cabinets, heads of state governments and party leaders.
Source: W. Zapf, *Wandlungen der deutschen Elite* (Munich, 1966), p. 180.

While the recruitment of the political elite in the Nazi era diverged from the European model, the way it developed in the Federal Republic was once again remarkably similar to that in other European countries. So far W.L. Guttsman is the only social scientist who has examined the change in the social origins of the politicians of the Federal Republic. He shows that in the Federal Republic, as in France and Great Britain, a decline in the number of politicians from the working class and a rapid increase in parliamentary deputies with higher education can be observed. The reasons for this development, however, remain to be investigated in detail.[18]

The small group of social scientists who, in the postwar period, have investigated the change in the social origins of political elites in Europe, have demonstrated that, after the opening up of these elites to the bourgeoisie and working class in the late nineteenth and early twentieth centuries, there has been, particularly in the postwar period, an opposite trend towards exclusiveness, towards a decline in the number of politicians from the working class in European parliaments and governments. To see this postwar trend as a return to the nineteenth century would, however, be to misunderstand fundamental developments. An increasing number of academically trained postwar politicians are professional politicians, whose careers are closely connected with party and interest group organisations and normally begin at a relatively early age at local level. The *embourgeoisement* of the left-wing parties, therefore, certainly does not represent a return to the honorary politicians of the nineteenth century. Also, in relation to the question which is central to this research report, namely the development of social mobility, the *embourgeoisement* of the European parliaments for various reasons does not mean a reversion to the inequality of opportunity characteristic of the nineteenth century. In the first place, the opportunities for upward mobility to workers in the early twentieth century through the left-wing parties in Europe were often exaggerated. The political elite (parliamentary deputies and leading party politicians) was always so small in numbers that it could offer the chance of social ascent to a minute proportion of workers or the sons of workers. The political careers in workers' parties, therefore, had a symbolic effect which may have influenced the concept of social mobility among workers; they scarcely altered the actual distribution of opportunities in the society of the late nineteenth and early twentieth centuries. Secondly, during the postwar period, a political career was no longer, as in the nineteenth century, virtually the only possibility of climbing out of the working class. To the marginal extent that we are concerned with here, the opportunities for the children of workers to move up into the upper ranks of the civil service, to become university teachers (and in some countries to secure top posts in industry) increased in postwar Europe to the same extent as the chances of workers following a political career decreased. Thirdly, and finally, the process of the *embourgeoisement* of the political elite appears to be limited to parliamentary deputies, ministers, and top party officials. The recruitment of trade union officials and of the vast mass of the party functionaries does not appear to reflect this tendency to the same degree. Here, avenues of advancement for political talent from the working class continued to remain open to the usual marginal extent.

Moreover, research on the process of *embourgeoisement* and of the formation of oligarchies within the political elite in postwar Europe left open a number of questions. First, the majority of authors see in this process not only or not so much a restriction on the opportunities for upward mobility of the working class, but rather the danger of the increasing alienation of the left-wing parties in Europe from a significant section of their voters, namely the working class. But it is on precisely this aspect of the political consequences of inequality of opportunity that up to now only fears have been expressed. There has been hardly any research on the question of how the change in the recruitment of the political elite has affected its political behaviour, on how the working-class voters have reacted to the shifts in the social origins of politicians. Secondly, the thesis of there having been an opening-up of the political elite in the late nineteenth and early twentieth centuries and the thesis of a growing tendency towards oligarchy in the postwar period are both based on very thin evidence. Basically, only the occupations and education of politicians have been investigated; in contrast to all the other fields of historical research on social mobility, however, the question of family background has almost invariably been ignored. It is not entirely clear how a more broadly based investigation would alter the thesis of a trend towards oligarchy. It could be that this thesis would be strengthened since the political elite in the early twentieth century came from only very narrow sections of the working class and since, in addition, the initial advantages and connexions provided by the family would become more apparent than hitherto. However, it could be that the thesis of a trend towards oligarchy would be weakened on the grounds that – as Johnson suspects and as Perkin has demonstrated for British ministers – a section of the academically-educated politicians are upwardly mobile and are distinguished from earlier politicians who came from the working class not so much on the basis of their family background as of their careers; they did not secure top political positions solely via trade unions and party organisations but, in addition, by acquiring a university education beforehand. Thirdly, so far there has been a complete dearth of comparative studies, whose main function would be not to elucidate regional and local differences but to explain the remarkable similarity of the trends in Western Europe.

6 APPENDIX : CONCEPTS AND INDICATORS

A whole range of concepts and indicators have been developed in sociological research on social mobility which, in many cases, are not immediately comprehensible, but which have demonstrated their utility and have also been employed to some extent in historical studies. Without an awareness of these concepts important arguments in the social science literature on social mobility are very difficult to follow. Thus, an attempt will be made to explain the most important of them.

Social mobility is itself a vague and theoretically ill-defined concept. One can understand it in very general terms to mean movements between social positions. But this definition is of very little use since it does not convey any idea of the actual goals of historical research on social mobility. In practice, the field of research termed 'social mobility' has in recent years acquired much more precise contours. Those outside the field often link two aspects with it which are, however, not necessarily dealt with in historical research: first, social mobility is not mostly concerned − as one might imagine − with the mobility of whole groups, such as the rise or decline of school teachers, or industrialists or of the nobility, but in general only with the mobility of individuals (individual mobility). Secondly, it is rare for geographical mobility or migration to be included under the term social mobility or, at any rate, they are rarely dealt with under this heading. The only works which also deal regularly with geographical mobility are those by American social historians. Otherwise there is a well-understood division of labour in which geographical mobility is primarily covered by demographic, sociogeographical, and urban studies, and on the other hand, social mobility is examined in close association with social stratification. In this more narrow field of social mobility, upward and downward mobility or − in more technical terms vertical mobility − is a prime focus of interest. There is, however, general agreement that every investigation of upward and downward mobility will provide points of controversy, either because it is rare to achieve a consensus about the definition of social stratification and class structure, or because (which is even more serious in historical studies) the quantifiable historical data on mobility necessary for complex attempts at the analysis of stratification or class are difficult to find. In this situation there are two solutions: either only simple kinds of social mobility which are easy to research are examined, or a highly simplified model of stratification and class identity is employed. In most cases both these solutions lead to the form of mobility which is most often used by historians – occupational mobility, i.e. movement between occupations. Information about occupations is relatively easy to come by and yet is very productive. At the moment, there is hardly a single historical work on social mobility which is not in practice a study of occupational mobility even if its focus is on the mobility between social strata and classes. In contrast, very few studies have dealt with income mobility or wealth mobility, i.e. movement between different income and wealth groups. Only a few American authors have so far succeeded in investigating how frequently individuals moved up or down between different wealth groups, whether this kind of mobility has increased or declined, and how far it was related to occupational mobility. Data on this are difficult to ascertain and tedious to use. Educational mobility, i.e. movement beteen levels of education, has also rarely been investigated. Here too data – with particular exceptions in higher education – are difficult to get hold of. Finally, historical investigations of prestige mobility, i.e. movement between social positions with different degrees of social prestige attached, are extremely rare since social science surveys on this aspect have not been carried out for a sufficient length of time, and substitute techniques have only been developed in a very crude form. Ideally, historical investigations of upward and downward social mobility should examine these various aspects of mobility in relation to each other.

The results of studies of mobility are influenced decisively by the kind of mobility which is being examined. Scholars differentiate between intergenerational mobility or mobility between generations and intragenerational mobility or career mobility. Those people are intergenerationally mobile whose career, status, or class differs from that of their parents or grandparents. Blue-collar workers whose fathers are graduates and white-collar employees whose fathers are peasants are intergenerationally mobile. If the career, status, or class remains the same between the generations the term used is *self-recruitment.* The bulk of studies on intergenerational mobility limit themselves to mobility between fathers and sons. Works which include female persons are just as rare as those which cover several generations. A favourite thesis of intergenerational mobility to the effect that social advance takes place over two or more generations has, therefore, rarely either been proved or disproved. The term intragenerational mobility or career mobility describes the change of career, status or class in the course of a person's occupational life. A skilled worker who advances to become a technician, a peasant who sells his land and becomes a construction worker, a shop assistant who marries a departmental manager — these are all intragenerationally mobile.

Social scientists also make a distinction which is very important for historical studies of social mobility between outflow and inflow. *Outflow* establishes what happens to the members of an occupational group (status group, or class) or their children. If one is interested in the question of how many workers become trade union or party functionaries or how many sons of industrialists become industrialists themselves, or how many daughters of artisans become graduates, one is raising the question of outflow. In contrast, *inflow* shows where the members of an occupational group, a stratum or class come from. If one investigates how often during the industrial revolution workers were downwardly mobile artisans, or how frequently professors came from the families of elementary school teachers, or how many millionaires had only an elementary education, one is dealing with inflow. This distinction is extremely important for studies of inequality of opportunity. This is demonstrated by the standard mobility table (see Table 6.1).

Each individual square of this two-dimensional standard table of social mobility contains three numbers: in the middle the absolute number, in the top right hand corner the outflow and in the bottom left hand corner the inflow. The outflow can be read off horizontally and the inflow vertically. In the case of the imaginary data in Table 6.1, two per cent of sons from the middle class moved up into the upper class and 34 per cent down into the lower class (outflow); on the other hand, 61 per cent of the fathers of the members of the middle class belonged to the upper class and 20 per cent to the lower class (inflow). At first sight, this distinction between inflow and outflow may appear artificial. But to show how necessary it is, this table was based on the unlikely case that the bulk of the members of the upper class had moved up from the lower class (80 per cent). The other assumptions of the imaginary data in Table 6.1 roughly correspond to German society round about 1900 (5 per cent upper class, 50 per cent lower class). Despite the assumption of a completely unreal openness of the upper class, only 9 per cent of the members of the lower class were able to move up into the upper class. If one only looks at the inflow, the upper class of this society appears very open; if one only looks at the outflow, it appears very closed. The decisive reason for this is the disproportionate size of these two strata. This example demonstrates

Table 6.1: Standard Mobility table*

Father's social class	Son's social class			Total	Number in sample	%
	Upper class	Middle class	Lower class			
Upper class	0% 1 1%	61% 160 17%	38% 100 10%	100%	261	14%
Middle class	2% 19 19%	64% 560 62%	34% 300 30%	100%	879	44%
Lower class	9% 80 80%	20% 180 20%	70% 600 60%	100%	860	43%
Total	100%	100%	100%			
Number in sample %	100 5%	900 45%	1000 50%		2000 100%	100%

*Data are imaginary.

that inflow and outflow can be distorted if the interpretation fails to take both kinds of mobility into consideration.

The standard mobility table (Table 6.1) contains further information. In the square in the bottom right hand corner one can read off the size of a random sample of a survey (in this case: 2000). The absolute numbers in each square provide an indication of how reliable the percentages are for a given sample. In this particular case, the absolute number of those self-recruited by the upper class is very small (a single case); this shows that the percentages are very unreliable. Finally, through the marginal distribution of the mobility table one can establish the social background of both the fathers and the sons. The term 'marginal distribution' refers to the extreme right hand column and the bottom line of the mobility matrix. The extreme right hand column defines the social background of the fathers, the bottom line the social background of the sons. Differences between these two marginal distributions indicate a historical change in the social background of these groups. In this particular, and admittedly not very realistic, case the percentage of the upper class declined from 14 per cent to 5 per cent, while the percentage of the lower class increased from 43 per cent to 50 per cent. The social structure of a society at a particular time can, however, only be assessed on the basis of the marginal distribution which has been founded on first-hand data. If, for example, Cologne marriage certificates of the year 1870 are used to discover the occupations of those who got married and of their fathers, and a mobility table illustrating intergenerational mobility is compiled on the basis of this evidence, it will elucidate the social structure of Cologne in 1870 (and even here only the social background of the inhabitants of marriageable age), but not the social structure of the previous generation, i.e. of around 1845. Marginal distributions can only indicate trends which are not subject to precise periodisation.

In historical research on social mobility there are two different kinds of investigation which are used in particular to analyse changes in social mobility: the most common type of investigation is the *comparison of surveys which have been carried out at different periods*. If surveys of American society in 1949, 1953, and 1958 are compared with one another, and if an historian compiles tables of career mobility for a city for the years 1860, 1870, and 1880 and compares them with each other, these are basically similar kinds of investigation. There are limits to what can be produced from historical comparisons – for technical reasons. At national level, they can normally only be carried out for the period after the Second World War because the sociological surveys on which they are based had not been carried out before then. For the earlier period this kind of investigation is almost invariably confined to local studies.[1] This disadvantage can be compensated for by *cohort analysis* (also called 'retrospective method'). It is based entirely on the data of contemporary mobility surveys, divides the interviewees into different age groups (cohorts), and assumes that the alterations in mobility rates between the older and younger age groups correspond to the historical changes in social mobility.[2] This method has the advantage of going back far into the past and of covering a period of up to a hundred years. There are, however, a number of reservations to be made. For the historian the most serious are: first, cohort analyses do not provide even an approximate picture of historical development if the frontiers of the particular country concerned are substantially altered or the composition of its population is significantly changed through migration. Both these are true of Germany, for example. Secondly, the data on which the cohort analyses are based consist, to a large extent, of statements by interviewees about the occupations and social status of their fathers and grandfathers, or about how they had placed themselves socially. This is the only way in which cohort analysis can go far back into the past. Undoubtedly, the interviewees either consciously or unconsciously make considerable errors in their statements. Above all, these statements are very difficult to evaluate and it is almost impossible to correct them subsequently. Undoubtedly, the greater the generation gap and the more the interviewers move from questions about occupation to those about social behaviour and social assessment, the more serious these mistakes become. Thus cohort analyses about prestige mobility in the nineteenth century are particularly unreliable. Thirdly, the historical evidence provided by cohort analyses carried out in the traditional manner is particularly inexact. Usually, only the date of birth and the date of the interview are known, while the much more important date (or age) at which the interviewees or their parents/grandparents had been mobile is unknown. Thus cohort analyses which are based solely on the birthdate only permit crude statements about trends. One cannot, for example, discover in which period a cohort which was born in 1895, most of whom presumably began their careers around 1910 and retired around 1960, and who were asked about their previous careers in 1970, moved up or down the social scale – in the interwar period and/or during the war and/or in the postwar period. On the basis of such cohort analyses, therefore, it is impossible to make comparisons between these three epochs; comparisons which a historian would find particularly interesting. As a result, it is not only impossible to make an accurate portrayal of the situation, but historical analysis in particular is virtually ruled out. One cannot investigate the effects on social mobility of political decisions and reforms, of wars, economic crises, periods of economic growth, changes in economic structure, population shifts etc. It should be said in defence of cohort analysis, however, that it is almost the only method which produces results for historical investigations of social mobility at national level before the Second World War. Moreover, a more thorough interrogation of the interviewees concerning the date at which they had been mobile would considerably improve cohort analysis and enable it to be utilised for historical studies.

A whole series of concepts and indicators have been specifically developed for the investigation of changes in social mobility, not all of which, however, have been used for historical research on social mobility. In the present state of research it seems appropriate to refer to at least four of these indicators.

(1) *Mobility ratios* (or the proportion of those who are mobile) show, in terms of occupational mobility, what proportion of all those covered by the survey did not continue in their original occupations or — in the case of intergenerational mobility — did not continue in the same occupation as their fathers. In the case of investigations of vertical mobility, the mobility ratio is comprised of the combination of the upward and downward mobility quotients. These indicators are normally employed in historical studies. It is precisely in the case of historical comparisons, however, that mobility quotients have a serious disadvantage, which they share with all other rates of social mobility (inflow and outflow), and which once again can be most effectively illustrated through a concrete example. If the rates of upward mobility of workers in non-manual occupations between 1850 and 1900 increased from 10 per cent to 15 per cent, this appears at first sight to represent a decrease in inequality of opportunity. But if, at the same time, the proportions of blue-collar and non-manual occupations altered so that the non-manual occupations increased sharply and the blue-collar occupations decreased sharply, then it could be that the rates of upward mobility for blue-collar workers only increased because there were more non-manual jobs available, without the non-manual jobs having become more accessible and without a higher proportion of non-manual employees coming from the working class. The crucial disadvantage of mobility ratios (and other mobility rates) is the fact that they do not take account of changes in the occupational and class structures.

(2) *Association indices* have been developed in order to take account of this. There are both simple and complicated versions of these. The

more simple form of association index (sometimes called a recruitment index) is used for investigations of social origins and is intended to take account of changes in the occupational structure. For example, if the number of farmers' children who enter secondary education declines, this does not necessarily mean a reduction in the opportunities for farmers' children of access to higher education. It could be that the reason for this is a decline in the proportion of farmers within the employed population. A number of examples of this association or recruitment index are shown in Table 6.2. The case of secondary

Table 6.2: The social origins of secondary school pupils in the German Reich (1931) and the Federal Republic (1965)

| Father's occupation | Germany (1931) | | Federal Republic (1965) | |
	% (1)	Association index (2)	% (3)	Association index (4)
Self-employed artisans, retailers, publicans	18	1.81	11	1.49
Farmers	5	0.62	3	0.85
White-collar employees	7	0.60	21	0.78
Workers	5	0.10	6	0.19

Source: H. Kaelble, 'Chancenungleichheit und akademische Ausbildung, 1910-1960', *Geschichte und Gesellschaft,* 1 (1975), pp. 142, 145.

school pupils from farming families is a particularly good example of the usefulness of this index. Thus, while their proportion fell between 1931 and 1965 from five per cent to three per cent — as is shown in Table 6.2 — the proportion of farmers in the employed population declined even more sharply. As a result, the association index rose; it shows that the opportunities for farmers' children of access to secondary schools had not decreased, but had actually improved slightly. To use this association index, one — to continue with this example — puts the proportion of students from farming families (S) in relation to the proportion of farmers among those employed (F) — (S:F). If this is below 1 — as for example is the case with the farmers' children — this represents discrimination. If it is 1, this means optimum equality of opportunity. In the case of comparisons, the change in the index is of greater importance: if the index rises, this represents an increasingly privileged status for those over 1 and decreasing discrimination for those below 1. If the index goes down, it is the other way round. This simple association index is a useful indicator for the historical comparison of the distribution of opportunities.

A more complicated and, for a long time, much more usual association index was developed by Natalie Rogoff for the mobility table already referred to. The basic idea is the same. It too was intended to take account of alterations in the occupational structure in historical comparisons of mobility rates. In the meantime, however, several sociologists have put forward serious objections to this association index on the grounds that in its present form it does not fulfill its function. It is, therefore, being used increasingly rarely in historical research on social mobility.[3]

(3) Another approach to the problem which the association index was intended to solve is provided by the distinction between *structural mobility* or enforced mobility and *circulation mobility*. The aim of this distinction is to distinguish mobility which is caused solely by changes in the occupational, status, or class structures, i.e. by social change, from mobility caused by other factors which really do constitute an 'open' society. If, for example, the occupational group formed by farmers contracts, this will cause mobility since either the farmers themselves or their sons will be moving into other occupational groups. If the occupational group formed by white-collar employees grows, this too will cause mobility since either these employees themselves or their fathers will have originally belonged to other occupational groups. The more decisive the changes in the social structure are, the more impact they will have on social mobility. The 'enforced' mobility caused by structural changes is called structural mobility. The other forms of mobility which do not derive from such structural changes are termed circulation mobility. As has been mentioned, the changes in the occupational or class structures can be read off the mobility table: one can work out from this the rate of structural mobility. Normally, structural mobility only forms part of the mobility process. One can work out the amount of circulation mobility by subtracting the rate of structural mobility from the mobility rate. In contrast to structural mobility, however, circulation mobility is a residual category. The reasons for its occurrence remain unclear.

Table 6.3 provides examples of structural and circulation mobility which Thernstrom worked out for late nineteenth and twentieth century Boston. From this table one can conclude that during the whole period only the smaller proportion of social mobility consisted of structural mobility and the larger proportion was circulation mobility. Moreover, the proportion of structural mobility declined slightly; the

importance of alterations in the occupational structure for social mobility in Boston appears, therefore, to have decreased somewhat. Circulation mobility increased slightly; this suggests a somewhat more open
society or one more geared to merit. These indicators are, of course,
only a crude basis for analysis. First, in the calculation of structural
mobility only those alterations in the occupational and status structures are taken into account which are analysed in that particular investigation and which are included in the mobility table. In the case of
Thernstrom's investigation, only the mobility between unskilled
workers (including semi-skilled), skilled workers, lower white-collar
and higher white-collar was investigated. Thus mobility between, for

Table 6.3: Mobility indicators for Boston 1840-1930

	Year of birth				
Indicators	1840-1959	1860-1879	1870-1889	ca. 1890-1930	1930
1. Observed (mobility rate) (%) mobility	54	56	56	51	52
2. Structural mobility (%)	23	23	20	17	11
3. Circulation mobility (3=1-2) (%)	31	33	36	34	41
4. Expected mobility (%)	76	76	74	74	72
5. Ratio of observed to expected mobility (5=1:4)	0.71	0.74	0.76	0.69	0.72

Source: S. Thernstrom, *The Other Bostonians* (Cambridge, Mass., 1973), p. 105.

example, self-employed artisans and non-supervisory white-collar occupations, or between various skilled blue-collar occupations was not
covered. If social mobility in Boston happened to be encouraged in
particular by the fact that the *petite bourgeoisie* had rapidly contracted
while the non-supervisory white collar occupations had rapidly expanded, this shift in the occupational structure would not be taken
account of in the investigation or be included in the structural mobility,
and this would, in turn, result in an erroneous picture of the extent of
the role played by other factors in the development of social mobility.
Secondly, in using these indicators one should bear in mind that the
estimation of structural mobility is based on very crude assumptions
about the effects of changes in the occupational and class structures; it
is assumed that mobile people from declining occupations transfer
directly to expanding occupations whereas, in reality, much more

complicated forms of movement are possible. To continue with the example used above: if agriculture declines and white-collar occupations increase in number, it is not necessarily the case that farmers immediately become white-collar employees. It is also possible for farmers to take up blue-collar jobs and for a larger proportion of blue collar workers to transfer to subordinate white-collar jobs. If one only observes the mobility between farmers and white-collar occupations, the effect of the change in the occupational structure appears, erroneously, to be very small. Despite these reservations, however, structural and circulation mobility can be useful indicators for historical research on social mobility.

(4) Another indicator which is used relatively frequently is provided by the *model of perfect mobility*. This model is based on the assumption that mobility is perfect if, in the case of intergenerational mobility, the distribution of sons corresponds solely with the structure of the fathers' and sons' occupations and otherwise is based on the law of probability. The same assumptions apply in the case of intragenerational mobility. For a given occupational structure one can work out mobility rates which (according to the model of perfect mobility) are described as *expected mobility*. The relationship between the mobility rate which is actually observed and the expected mobility rate is a further indicator of social mobility. This indicator too has the advantage of taking account of changes in the occupational and class structures. It measures the actual mobility against a standard of perfect mobility which is normally intended simply for heuristic purposes. This indicator moves between 0 and 1. If it goes down, it implies increasing immobility; if it goes up it implies increasing mobility. Table 6.3 also contains examples of this indicator. As one can see from the bottom line, in the case of Boston the indicator was quite high. It varies but does not show any clear-cut trend and, thereby, confirms Thernstrom's main thesis, namely that in late nineteenth and twentieth century Boston social mobility remained steady at a high level. When using this indicator too, one must bear in mind a number of points: first, like other indicators it depends to a large extent on the way the investigation is set up. It only permits comparisons if the investigations being compared are set up in a similar fashion. It will not provide information about mobility processes which are not covered by the investigation. Secondly, like all indicators in the social sciences, it has the disadvantage that the complex mobility processes of a whole society are contained in a single figure. This facilitates a rapid survey. But, in order to secure a more penetrating interpretation, it is essential to see

the mobility rate in the context of the complex data which it summarises.

Apart from these four mobility indicators, which are the ones most frequently used, sociologists have developed a whole series of further indicators. They represent technical improvements on the two indicators referred to last, but so far have only been used occasionally in historical research on social mobility. The most comprehensive assessment and the most incisive discussion of them has been undertaken by Raymond Boudon.[4] All these indicators, however, are mainly appropriate for the description of the development of social mobility. They do not contribute much to its analysis. For this purpose two techniques in particular have been developed since the Second World War: *path analysis*, which has been successfully used by Christopher Jencks and Walter Müller[5] for contemporary investigations of equality of opportunity in the educational sector, and the *Markov-Chains*. Hitherto, as far as is known, neither path analysis nor Markov-Chains have been used in a historical study of social mobility. In the case of path analysis, in particular, this should only be a question of time, of the availability of sources, of the spread of statistical expertise among historians, or the broadening of historical interest among sociologists.[6]

NOTES

1. Introduction

1. This report is restricted to historical research since a number of good general surveys of research on social mobility have appeared recently: cf. K. Macdonald & J. Ridge, 'Social Mobility' in A.H. Halsey (ed.), *Trends in British Society since 1900* (London, 1972); J. Bibby, 'Social Mobility 1960-1975', *Current Sociology*, 24 (1976); B.A. Dietrick, 'Social Mobility: 1969-1973', *Annals of the American Academy of Political and Social Sciences*, 414 (1974); K.U. Mayer, 'Soziale Mobilität' in E.R. Wiehn & K.U. Mayer (eds.), *Soziale Schichtung und Mobilität* (München, 1975); K.M. Bolte & H. Recker, 'Vertikale Mobilität' in R. König (ed.), *Handbuch der empirischen Sozialforschung*, 2nd edn, vol. 5, (Stuttgart, 1976); H. Recker, *Mobilität in der "offenen" Gesellschaft*, (Köln, 1974); S. Kirchberger, *Kritik der Schichtungs- und Mobilitätsforschung* (Frankfurt, 1975). Furthermore, this report deals only with recent research and is, therefore, not a comprehensive bibliographical essay. Finally, while this research report demonstrates very clearly the need for and the possibility of comparative international research in the field of the history of social mobility, it does not itself draw such comparisons. I will publish my own views on this question elsewhere. Reference is made to this in the relevant notes.

2. This will be the topic of another research survey which I hope to publish in 1981 (in German).

3. Parallel to this report a collection of the most important essays on the history of social mobility in the nineteenth and twentieth centuries was published (cf. H. Kaelble (ed.) *Geschichte der sozialen Mobilität seit der industriellen Revolution* (Königstein, Hain 1978).

2. The Trend of Social Mobility

1. G. Pourcher, 'Un essai d'analyse par cohorte de la mobilité géographique et professionelle en France', *Acta Sociologica*, 9 (1965), pp. 144 ff.; G. Kleining, 'Die Veränderung der Mobilitätschancen in der Bundesrepublik Deutschland *Kölner Zeitschrift für Soziologie und Socialpsychologie*, 23 (1971); 'Soziale Mobilität in der Bundesrepublik Deutschland, I: Klassenmobilität', ibid., 27 (1975); J.C. Goyder & J.E. Curtis, 'A Three-Generational Approach to Trends in Occupational Mobility', *American Journal of Sociology*, 81 (1975); G. Carlsson, *Social Mobility and Class Structure* (Lund, 1958), p. 90. On the concept of 'retrospective method' see the last chapter.

2. H. van Dijk, *Rotterdam 1810-1880. Aspecten van een stedelijke samenleving* (Schiedam, 1976), pp. 132ff, 143ff; H. van Dijk, 'De beroepsmobiliteit in Rotterdam in de negentiende eeuw', in J. van Herwaarden (ed.), *Lof der historie* (Rotterdam, 1974); R. Mayntz, *Soziale Schichtung und sozialer Wandel in einer Industriegemeinde* (Stuttgart, 1958), pp. 75ff; H.J. Daheim, 'Berufliche Intergenerationen-Mobilität in der komplexen Gesellschaft', *Kölner Zeitschrift für Soziologie und Sozialpsychologie*, 16 (1964) p. 99.

3. W.L. Warner & P.S. Lunt, *The Social Life of a Modern Community* (New Haven, 1941), p. 90f.

125

4. S. Thernstrom, *Poverty and Progress. Social Mobility in a Nineteenth Century City* (Cambridge, 1964), pp. 80ff; S. Thernstrom, 'Yankee City Revisted: The Perils of Historical Naivety', *American Sociological Review* (1965); P.R. Knights, *The Plain People of Boston 1830-1860* (New York, 1971), pp. 85ff; S. Blumin, 'Mobility and Change in Ante-Bellum Philadelphia', in S. Thernstrom & R. Sennett (eds.), *Nineteenth Century Cities* (New Haven/London 1969), pp. 180ff, 200ff; C. Griffen, 'Making it in America: Social Mobility in Mid-Nineteenth Century Poughkeepsie', *New York History*, 51 (1970), pp. 481ff; C. Griffen & S. Griffen, *Natives and Newcomers: the Ordering of Opportunities in Mid-Nineteenth Century Poughkeepsie* (Cambridge, Mass., 1978); R.J. Hopkins, 'Occupational and Geographic Mobility in Atlanta, 1870 to 1896', *Journal of Southern History*, 34 (1968); M.B. Katz, *The People of Hamilton, Canada West: Family and Class in a Mid-Nineteenth Century City* (Cambridge, Mass., 1975). On further studies of the history of the USA see: J. Modell, "Die "Neue Sozialgeschichte" in Amerika', *Geschichte und Gesellschaft*, 1 (1975); R.S. Alcorn & P.R. Knights, 'Most Uncommon Bostonians', *Historical Methods Newsletter*, 8 (1975).

5. T. Rishoy, 'Metropolitan Social Mobility 1850-1950. The Case of Copenhagen', *Quality and Quantity*, 5 (1971).

6. P. Aycoberry, 'Probleme der Sozialschichtung in Köln im Zeitalter der Frühindustrialisierung', in W. Fischer (ed.), *Wirtschafts- und sozialgeschichtliche Probleme der frühen Industrialisierung* (Berlin, 1968), pp. 512ff.; L. Beutin, 'Euskirchens Wirtschaft in 19. und 20. Jahrhundert', in *650 Jahre Stadt Euskirchen 1302-1952* (Euskirchen, 1952), pp. 287ff.

7. On this see the numerous points raised in: R. Braun 'Historische Demographie im Rahmen einer integrierten Geschichtsbetrachtung', *Geschichte und Gesellschaft*, 3 (1977); also, P.A. Sorokin, *Social and Cultural Mobility in Industrial Society* (Glencoe, 1959), pp. 215ff.

8. Cf. S. Thernstrom, 'Class and Mobility in a 19th Century City', in R. Bendix & S.M. Lipset (eds.), *Class, Status and Power* (New York, 1966), pp. 603ff.

9. Cf. F.F. Mendels, 'Social Mobility and Phases of Industrialization and Social Mobility', *Journal of Interdisciplinary History*, 7 (1976). See also the following chapter on opportunities for social elevation among the working class.

10. For a summary see, Carlsson, *Social Mobility and Class Structure*, p. 106.

11. T. Geiger, 'Soziale Umschichtungen in einer dänischen Mittelstadt', *Acta Jutlandica* vol., 23, 1 (Kopenhagen, 1951), pp. 109ff.

12. N. Rogoff, *Recent Trends in Occupational Mobility* (Glencoe, 1953); D.V. Glass & J.R. Hall, 'Social Mobility in Great Britain: A Study of Inter-Generational Changes in Status', in D.V. Glass, *Social Mobility in Britain* (London, 1954); Carlsson, *Social Mobility and Class Structure*, pp. 90ff; J.J.M. van Tulder, *De beroepsmobiliteit in Nederland van 1919 tot 1954*, (Leiden, 1952), pp. 94ff; J.J.M. van Tulder, *Occupational Mobility in the Netherlands 1919 to 1954, Transactions of the 3rd World Congress of Sociology*, vol. 3 (London, 1956) p. 214; Rishoy, 'Metropolitan Social Mobility'; S. Thernstrom, *The Other Bostonians; Poverty and Progress in the American Metropolis 1880-1970* (Cambridge, 1973); H.P. Chudacoff, *Mobile Americans, Residential and Social Mobility in Omaha, 1880 to 1920*, (New York, 1972); G. Kleining, 'Struktur- und Prestigemobilität in der Bundesrepublik Deutschland', *Kölner Zeitschrift für Soziologie*, 23 (1971); J. Marceau, 'Education and social mobility in France' in F. Parkin (ed.), *The Social Analysis of Class Structure* (London, 1974); J. Marceau, *Class and Status in France: Economic Change and Social Immobility 1945-1975* (Oxford, 1977); R. Boudon, *Education, Opportunity and Social Inequality. Changing Prospects in Western Society* (New York, 1973), pp. 168ff.

13. P.M. Blau & O. Duncan, *The American Occupational Structure*, (New York, 1967), pp. 81ff; R.M. Hauser *et al.*, 'Structural Changes in Occupational

Mobility among Men in the United States', *American Sociological Review*, 40
(1975); S. Goldstein, *Patterns of Mobility, 1910-1950: The Norristown Study*
(Philadelphia, 1958), pp. 169ff; J.C. Tully, E.F. Jackson & R.F. Curtis, 'Trends in
Occupational Mobility in Indianapolis', *Social Forces*, 49 (1970/71).

14. A. Darbel, 'L'Évolution récente de la mobilité sociale', *Economie et statistique*, 71, Oct. 1975, pp. 18f; Pourcher, 'Un essai d'analyse par cohorte de la
mobilité géographique et professionelle en France', pp. 144ff. Unfortunately, the
cohort analysis used for the surveys of 1964 and 1972 was not applied either for
intergenerational or for intragenerational mobility. Cf. M. Praderie & M. Passagez,
'La Mobilité professionelle en France entre 1959 et 1964', *Etudes et conjoncture*,
vol. 21, 10 (1966); ibid., vol. 22, 2 (1967); R. Pohl *et al*., 'L'enquête formation-
qualification de 1970', *Les collections de l'INSEE*, vol. D. 32, (1974). On the state
of research in France see, G. Dupeux, 'L'Etude de la mobilité sociale', *Conjoncture économique, structures sociales* (Paris, 1974).

15. K. Svalastoga, *Prestige, Class and Mobility* (Copenhagen, 1959), pp. 349ff;
J.H. Goldthorpe, C. Llewellyn & C. Payne, *Social Mobility and Class Structure in
Modern Britain* (Oxford, 1980), pp. 68ff.

16. See the debate between Gerhard Kleining, Karl Ulrich Mayer and Walter
Müller in the *Kölner Zeitschrift für Soziologie*, 23, 1972 and 24, 1973; also K.U.
Mayer & W. Müller, 'Progress in Social Mobility Research?' *Quality and Quantity*,
5 (1971); K.U. Mayer, 'Recent Developments in the Opportunity Structure of
(West-) German Society 1955-1971', unpublished manuscript (very important
both methodologically and in terms of its content).

17. H. Kaelble, 'Soziale Mobilität in Deutschland, 1900-1960' in H. Kaelble
et al., Probleme der Modernisierung in Deutschland (Opladen, 1978); H. Kaelble,
'Social Mobility in Germany, 1900-1960', *Journal of Modern History*, 50 (1978);
G. Kleining, 'Soziale Mobilität in der Bundesrepublik Deutschland', *Kölner Zeitschrift für Soziologie*, 27 (1975), pp. 115ff, 287ff; K.M. Bolte, *Sozialer Aufstieg
und Abstieg* (Stuttgart, 1959), pp. 137ff, 213ff.

18. Carlsson, *Social Mobility and Class Structure*, p. 108f; J.M. Ridge, 'Fathers
and Sons' in J.M. Ridge (ed.) *Mobility in Britain Reconsidered* (Oxford, 1974);
O.D. Duncan, D.L. Featherman & B. Duncan, *Socioeconomic Background and
Achievement* (New York, London, 1972), pp. 37ff; R. Boudon, *Education, Opportunity and Social Inequality* (New York, 1973), pp. 153ff; see also, W. Müller,
Familie, Schule und Beruf (Opladen, 1975); R. Girod, *Milieu social et orientation
de la carrière des adolescents* (Geneva, 1962); W. Müller & K.U. Mayer, *Chancengleichheit durch Bildung* (Stuttgart, 1976).

19. Goldthorpe *et al., Social Mobility*, pp. 68ff.; Darbel, 'L'Évolution récente
de la mobilité sociale', pp. 18ff; P.M. Blau & O.D. Duncan, *The American Occupational Structure* (New York, 1967), pp. 428ff.

3. Opportunities for Upward Mobility among Industrial Workers

1. For a very good review of the history of the various theoretical approaches
to social mobility see John H. Goldthorpe *et al., Social Mobility and Class Structure in Modern Britain* (Oxford, 1980), pp. 3ff.

2. S. Thernstrom, *Poverty and Progress. Social Mobility in a Nineteenth
Century City* (Cambridge, 1964); see also the summary in Thernstrom, 'Class and
Mobility in a Nineteenth-Century City; A study of Unskilled Laborers' in
R.Bendix & S.M. Lipset (eds.), *Class, Status and Power*, 2nd edn (New York,
1966). For his own later assessment of this book see Thernstrom, 'Working-Class
Social Mobility in Industrial America', in M. Richter (ed.), *Essays in Theory and*

History (Cambridge, 1970); S. Blumin, 'Mobility and Change in Ante-Bellum Philadelphia' in S. Thernstrom & R. Sennett (eds.), *Nineteenth-Century Cities* (New Haven, 1969); P.R. Knights, *The Plain People of Boston 1830-1860* (New York, 1971), pp. 91ff: H.P. Chudacoff, *Mobile Americans: Residential and Social Mobility in Omaha 1880-1920* (New York, 1972), pp. 96ff; C. Griffen, 'Workers Divided: The Effect of Craft and Ethnic Differences in Poughkeepsie, New York, 1850-1880' in Thernstrom & Sennett (eds.), *Nineteenth-Century Cities*; Griffen, 'Making it in America: Social Mobility in Mid Nineteenth-Century Poughkeepsie', *New York History*, 51 (1970); A. Dawley, *Class and Community*, (Cambridge, 1976), pp. 159ff; R.J. Hopkins, 'Occupational and Geographic Mobility in Atlanta 1870-1896', *Journal of Southern History*, 34, 1968; P.B. Worthman, 'Working Class Mobility in Birmingham, Alabama, 1880-1914' in T.K. Hareven (ed.), *Anonymous Americans* (Engelwood Cliffs, 1971); D.R. Esslinger, *Immigrants and the City: Ethnicity and Mobility in a 19th Century Midwestern Community*, (Port Washington, 1975); D.T. Kearns, 'The Social Mobility of New Orleans Labourers 1870-1900', unpublished PhD thesis, Tulane University, 1977; J. Bodnar, *Immigration and Industrialization: Ethnicity in an American Mill Town, 1870-1940*, (Pittsburgh, 1977).

3. See in particular S. Thernstrom, *The Other Bostonians: Poverty and Progress in the American Metropolis 1880-1970* (Cambridge, 1973) pp. 220-61.

4. A second problem was the fact that some of the self-employed had lower and less secure incomes than skilled workers and thus the change from being a dependent worker to having a self-employed career by no means always represented a social advance but could be a way out for unemployed workers during economic crises. Griffen refers to this problem. For this reason studies of Britain, which we shall return to, include a section of the self-employed among the working class. Similar problems exist for the lower ranks of white-collar employees.

5. D. Bythell, *The Handloom Weavers. A Study in the English Cotton Industry during the Industrial Revolution*, (Cambridge, 1969), pp. 257ff.; M. Sanderson, 'Literacy and Social Mobility in the Industrial Revolution', *Past and Present*, 56 (1972); the discussion which followed between T.W. Wagener and M. Sanderson in *Past and Present* , 64, (1974); M. Anderson, *Family Structure in 19th Century Lancashire* (Cambridge, 1971), pp. 28ff, 120ff. (Anderson is currently engaged on a project on the social structure of London in the mid-nineteenth century which will also investigate social mobility.); E.J. Hobsbawm, 'The Labor Aristocracy in Nineteenth-Century Britain' in P.N. Stearns & D. Walkowitz, (eds.), *Workers in the Industrial Revolution* (New Brunswick, 1974), pp. 160f; J.F.C. Harrison, *Learning and Living, 1790-1960* (London, 1961), pp. 203ff; Harrison, *The Early Victorians 1832-1851* (London, 1971), pp. 135ff, T.R. Tholfsen, *Working-Class Radicalism in Mid-Victorian England* (London, 1976), pp. 222ff, 308ff; G. Crossick, 'The Labour Aristocracy and its Values: A Study of Mid-Victorian Kentish London', *Victorian Studies* 19, (1976), pp. 306f; R.Q. Gray, 'Thrift and Working-Class Mobility in Victorian Edinburgh' in A.A. Maclaren (ed.), *Social Class in Scotland* (Edinburgh, 1976). See also G. Crossick, *An Artisan Elite in Victorian Society. Kentish London 1840-1880*, (London, 1978), pp. 105ff.

6. P. Pierrard, *La Vie Ouvrière à Lille sous le Second Empire* (Paris, 1965), pp. 354ff; W.H. Sewell, 'Social Mobility in a Nineteenth-Century European City', *Journal of Interdisciplinary History*, 7 (1976); Theresa McBride, *The Domestic Revolution: The Modernization of Household Service in England and France 1820-1920* (London, 1976), pp. 90ff; R. Trempé, *Les Mineurs de Carmaux 1848-1914* (Paris, 1971), vol. 1, pp. 115ff, 169ff, 317ff; J.W. Scott, *The glassworkers of Carmaux* (Cambridge, 1974) pp. 35ff, 72ff, 168ff; Y. Lequin, 'La

formation du prolétariat industriel dans la région lyonnaise au XIXe siècle', *Le mouvement social*, 97 (1976), pp. 129ff; Lequin, *Les Ouvriers de la région lyonnaise dans la seconde moitié du XIXe siècle, 1848-1914*, (Lyon, 1977); S. Chassagne, A. Dewerpe & Y. Gaulupeau, 'Les ouvriers de la manufacture de toiles imprimées d'Oberkampf à Jouy-en-Josas (1760-1815)', *Le mouvement social*, 97 (1976), pp. 77ff; D. Woronoff, 'Le monde ouvrier de la sidérurgie ancienne', ibid., pp. 113ff; G. Hardach, *Der soziale Status des Arbeiters in der Frühindustrialisierung. Eine Untersuchung über die Arbeitnehmer in der französischen eisenschaffenden Industrie zwischen 1800 und 1870* (Berlin 1969), pp. 62ff. See also, A. Corbin, 'La Mobilité sociale en France au 19e siècle', unpublished paper 1979.

 7. F.D. Marquardt, 'Sozialer Aufstieg, sozialer Abstieg und die Entstehung der Berliner Arbeiterklasse, 1806-1848', *Geschichte und Gesellschaft*, 1 (1975); Marquardt, 'A Working Class in Berlin in the 1840s', in H.-U. Wehler, *Sozialgeschichte Heute. Festschrift für Hans Rosenberg* (Göttingen, 1974); P. Lundgreen, *Techniker in Preussen während der frühen Industrialisierung*, (Berlin, 1975), pp. 85ff; H. Zwahr, *Zur Konstituierung des Proletariats als Klasse Strukturuntersuchungen über das Leipziger Proletariat während der industriellen Revolution*, (Berlin, 1978); D. Crew, 'Definition of Modernity: Social Mobility in a German Town, 1880-1901', *Journal of Social History*, 7 (1973); L. Niethammer, 'Wie wohnten die Arbeiter im Kaiserreich', *Archiv für Sozialgeschichte*, 16 (1977); R. Mayntz, *Soziale Schichtung und sozialer Wandel in einer Industriegemeinde*, (Stuttgart, 1958), pp. 146ff; H.J. Daheim, 'Berufliche Intergenerationen-Mobilität in der komplexen Gesellschaft', *Kölner Zeitschrift für Soziologie*, 16 (1964); H. Pohl (ed.), *Arbeiterfragen im Industrialisierungsprozeß* (Stuttgart, 1978). See also W. Conze & U. Engelhardt (eds.), *Arbeiterfragen im Industrialisierungsprozess* (Stuttgart, 1979), (articles by P. Borscheid, H.-J. Rupieper, H. Schomerus, W. Hippel, K. Ditt, K. Tenfelde); J. Kocka, 'The Study of Social Mobility and the Formation of the Working Class in the 19th Century' in *Le mouvement social* (forthcoming); R. Vetterli, *Industriearbeit, Arbeiterbewusstsein und gewerkschaftliche Organisation. Dargestellt am Beispiel der Georg Fischer AG (1890-1930)* (Göttingen, 1978). Older post-war studies, most of which only briefly touch on the social mobility of industrial workers and do not examine them empirically and in depth are being taken account of in the recent investigations and are, therefore, not referred to again here. The numerous case studies from the pre-1914 period are also not dealt with here since they require a separate thorough and critical analysis by a social historian.

 8. J. Kocka, 'Industrielle Angestelltenschaft in frühindustrieller Zeit', in O. Büsch (ed.), *Untersuchungen zur Geschichte der frühen Industrialisierung vornehmlich im Wirtschaftsraum Berlin/Brandenburg* (Berlin, 1971), pp. 342f; E. Glovka-Spencer, 'Between Capital and Labor:Supervisory Personnel in Ruhr Heavy Industry before 1914', *Journal of Social History*, 9 (1975), pp. 181ff; K. Tenfelde, *Sozialgeschichte der Bergarbeiterschaft an der Ruhr im 19. Jh.'* (Bonn-Bad Godesberg, 1977), pp. 246ff, p. 339; H. Kaelble, 'Soziale Mobilität in Deutschland, 1900-1960', in *Probleme der Modernisierung in Deutschland*, (Opladen, 1978); R. Mayntz, *Soziale Schichtung und sozialer Wandel in einer Industriegemeinde* (Stuttgart, 1958); H. Daheim, 'Berufliche Intergenerationen-Mobilität in der komplexen Gesellschaft', *Kölner Zeitschrift für Soziologie und Sozialpsychologie*, 16 (1964).

 9. H. Schomerus, 'Ausbildung und Aufstiegsmöglichkeiten württembergischer Metallarbeiter 1850 bis 1914 am Beispiel der Maschinenfabrik Esslingen', in U. Engelhardt, V. Sellin & H. Stuke (eds.) *Soziale Bewegung und politische Verfassung* (Stuttgart, 1976); P.N. Stearns, *Lives of Labour*, (London, 1976),

pp. 336ff; P. Borscheid & H. Schomerus, 'Mobilität und soziale Lage der württembergischen Fabrikarbeiterschaft im 19. Jahrhundert', in P.J. Müller (ed.), *Die Analyse prozess-orientierter Daten* (Stuttgart, 1977); P. Borscheid, *Textilarbeiterschaft in der Industrialisierung* (Stuttgart, 1978); H. Schomerus, *Die Arbeiter der Maschinenfabrik Esslingen. Forschungen zur Lage der Arbeiterschaft im 19. Jahrhundert* (Stuttgart, 1977).

4. The Development of Equality of Opportunity in the Education Sector

1. N. Hans, *New Trends in Education in the Eighteenth Century* (London, 1951), pp. 43ff, 210f; C.A. Anderson & M. Schnaper, *School and Society in England: Social Background of Oxford and Cambridge Students* (Washington, 1951); T.W. Bamford, 'Public Schools and Social Class, 1801-1850', *British Journal of Sociology*, 12 (1961), pp. 225ff; B. Simon, *Studies in the History of Education 1780-1870* (London, 1960), pp. 298ff; a collection of the older and less empirically soundly-based opinions in E.G. West, *Education and the Industrial Revolution* (London, 1975), pp. 3ff.

2. S. Rothblatt, *The Revolution of the Dons: Cambridge and Society in Victorian England* (London, 1968), pp. 29ff; J. Lawson & H. Silver, *History of Education in England* (London, 1973), pp. 337ff; L. Stone, 'The Size and Composition of the Oxford Student Body 1580-1910', in Stone (ed.), *The University in Society*, vol. 1, (Princeton, 1974), pp. 37ff, 65ff. A parallel study of Cambridge unfortunately let slip the opportunity of investigating the historical change in the social origins of the students (see H. Jenkins & D.C. Jones, 'Social Class of Cambridge University Alumni of the 18th and 19th Centuries', *British Journal of Sociology*, 1 (1950).

3. W. Zorn, 'Hochschule und höhere Schule in der deutschen Sozialgeschichte der Neuzeit', in K. Repgen & S. Skalweit (eds.), *Spiegel der Geschichte* (Münster, 1964); K.H. Jarausch, 'Die neuhumanistische Universität und die bürgerliche Gesellschaft 1800-1870', *Vierteljahrschrift für Sozial- und Wirtschaftsgeschichte* (1978); Jarausch, 'The Sources of German Student Unrest, 1815-1848' in L. Stone (ed.), *The University in Society* (Princeton, 1975), pp. 522ff; P. Lundgreen, *Techniker in Preussen während der frühen Industrialisierung* (Berlin, 1975), pp. 119f; Lundgreen, 'Technicians and the Labour Market in Prussia, 1810-1850', *Annales Cisalpines d'Histoire Sociale*, 2 (1971), pp. 13ff; M. Kraul, 'Untersuchungen zur sozialen Struktur der Schülerschaft des preussischen Gymnasiums im Vormärz', *Bildung und Erziehung*, 29 (1976), p. 516; F. Ringer, 'Higher Education in Germany in the 19th Century', *Journal of Contemporary History*, 2 (1967), pp. 132ff; Ringer, *Education and Society* (Bloomington, 1979); K.H. Jarausch, 'The Social Transformation of the University in the Case of Prussia 1865-1914', *Journal of Social History*, 12 (1979/80); J. Kocka, 'Bildung, soziale Schichtung und soziale Mobilität im deutschen Kaiserreich am Beispiel der gewerblich-technischen Ausbildung', in B.J. Wendt, D. Stegmann and P.-C. Witt (eds.), *Industrielle Gesellschaft und politisches System* (Bonn, 1978); H. Titze, *Die Politisierung der Erziehung* (Frankfurt, 1973); D.K. Müller, *Sozialstruktur und Schulsystem. Aspekte zum Strukturwandel des 19. Jahrhunderts* (Göttingen, 1977), pp. 55ff, 154ff, 521ff; P. Lundgreen, 'Die Bildungschancen bei Übergang von der "Gesamtschule" zum Schulsystem der Klassengesellschaft im 19. Jahrhundert', *Zeitschrift für Pädogogik*, 24 (1978); see also, H.-G. Herrlitz & H. Titze, (Überfüllung als bildungspolitische Strategie, Zur administrativen Steuerung der Lehrerarbeitslosigkeit in Preussen 1870-1914' in U. Herrmann (ed.), *Schule und Gesellschaft im 19. Jahrhundert* (Weinheim, 1977), pp. 359ff; being pub-

lished: P. Koppenhöfer, 'Höhere Bildung und Auslese. Untersuchungen zur sozialen Herkunft der höheren Schüler Badens 1834/36-1890' (PhD thesis, Heidelberg, 1977); M. Kraul, *Gymnasium und Gesellschaft im Vormärz* (Göttingen, 1980); H. Kaelble, 'Educational Opportunities and Government Policies: Post-Primary European Education before 1914, in P. Flora & A.J. Heidenheimer (eds.), *The Development of the Welfare State in Europe* (New Brunswick, 1980).

4. H. Chisick, 'Bourses d'études et mobilité sociale en France à la veille de la révolution', *Annales*, 30 (1975); W. Frijhoff & D. Julia, *Ecole et société dans la France d'ancien régime* (Paris, 1975); R. Anderson, 'Secondary Education in Mid-Nineteenth-Century France', *Past & Present*, 53 (1971); Anderson, 'The Conflict in Education. Catholic Secondary Schools (1850-1870): A Reappraisal', in T. Zeldin (ed.), *Conflicts in French Society* (London, 1970), pp. 70-3 (now in Anderson, *Education in France 1848-1870* (Oxford, 1975)); C.R. Day, 'Technical and Professional Education in France: The Rise and Fall of l'enseignement secondaire spéciale, 1865-1902', *Journal of Social History*, 6 (1973/74); P.J. Harrigan, 'Secondary Education and the Professions in France during the Second Empire', *Comparative Studies in Society and History*, 17 (1975): Harrigan, 'The social origins, ambitions, and occupations of secondary students in France during the Second Empire', in L. Stone (ed.), *Schooling and Society. Studies in the History of Education* (Baltimore, 1976); M. Lévy-Leboyer, 'Le Patronat francais a-t-il été malthusien?' *Le mouvement social*, 88 (1974), pp. 18ff; F. Ringer, *Education and Society* (Bloomington, 1979).

5. M. Mathew, 'The Origins and Occupations of Glasgow Students, 1740-1839', *Past & Present*, 33 (1966); J. Scotland, *The History of Scottish Education*, vol. 1 (London, 1969), pp. 333f. (Workers' sons at the University of Glasgow 1866/67, 21 per cent.)

6. For France see, P. Bourdieu, 'Avenir de classe et causalité du probable', *Revue française de sociologie*, 15 (1974); Bourdieu, Les stratégies de reconversion, les classes sociales et le systeme d'enseignement', *Information sur les sciences sociales*, 12 (1973); J. Marceau, 'Education and Social Mobility in France', in Frank Parkin (ed.), *The Social Analysis of Class Structure* (London, 1974); C. Peyre, 'L'Origine sociale des élèves de l'enseignement secondaire en France' in P. Naville (ed.), *Ecole et Société* (Paris 1959). For the USA see the research surveys: Sol Cohen, 'The History of the History of American Education, 1900-1976: The Uses of the Past', *Harvard Educational Review*, 46 (1976); D. Sloan, 'Historiography and the History of Education', *Review of Research in Education*, 1 (1973). One of the few historical investigations of the distribution of opportunities in American education (apart from studies of black Americans and immigrants is Carl F. Kaestle, *The Evolution of an Urban School System* (Cambridge, 1973).

7. J.E. Floud, A.H. Halsey & F.M. Martin, *Social Class and Educational Opportunity* (Melbourne, London, Toronto, 1956) (reprinted London 1972); see also, J. Floud, 'Social Class Factors in Educational Achievement', in A.H. Halsey (ed.), *Ability and Educational Opportunity* (Paris, 1961) (reprinted in M. Craft (ed.), *Family, Class, and Education*, (London, 1970)); A. Little & J. Westergaard, 'The Trend of Class Differentials in Educational Opportunity in England and Wales', *British Journal of Sociology*, 15 (1964); see also, John Westergaard & A. Little, 'Educational Opportunity and Social Selection in England and Wales: Trends and Policy Implications', in M. Craft (ed.), *Family, Class and Education* (London, 1970); A.H. Halsey, J. Sheehan & J. Vaizey, 'Schools' in A.H. Halsey, (ed.), *Trends in British Society since 1900* (London, 1972), pp. 161f; A. Halsey, 'Higher Education' in ibid. p. 204; A.J. Heidenheimer & M. Parkinson, 'Equalizing Educational Opportunity in Britain and the United States' in W.E. Gwyn & G. Edwards (eds.), *Perspectives on Public Policy Making* (New Orleans, 1975); A.H. Halsey,

'Towards Meritocracy?' 'The Case of Britain' in J. Karabel & A.H. Halsey (eds.), *Power and Ideology in Education* (New York, 1977).

8. See with reference to further literature: W. Zorn, 'Hochschule und höhere Schule in der deutschen Sozialgeschichte der Neuzeit' in K. Repgen & S. Skalweit (eds.), *Spiegel der Geschichte* (Münster, 1964); H. Kaelble, 'Chancenungleichheit und akademische Ausbildung in Deutschland 1910-1960', *Geschichte und Gesellschaft*, 1 (1975); H. Milberg, *Schulpolitik in der pluralistischen Gesellschaft* (Hamburg, 1970), pp. 168ff; H. Giesecke, 'Zur Schulpolitik der Sozialdemokraten in Preussen und im Reich 1918/19', *Vierteljahrshefte für Zeitgeschichte*, 13 (1965); D. Hagener, *Radikale Schulreform zwischen Programmatik und Realität. Die schulpolitischen Kämpfe vor dem ersten Weltkrieg und in der Enstehungsphase der Weimarer Republik* (Bremen, 1973); M.H. Kater, *Studentenschaft und Rechtsradikalismus in Deutschland 1918-1933* (Hamburg, 1975), pp. 56ff; W. Kreutzberger *Studenten und Politik 1918-1933. Der Fall Freiburg im Breisgau* (Göttingen, 1972), pp. 52ff; D. Schoenbaum, *Hitler's Social Revolution* (New York, 1967), pp. 261ff; D. Orlow, 'Die Adolf-Hitler-Schulen', *Vierteljahrshefte für Zeitgeschichte*, 13 (1965); J. McIntyre (now Stephenson), 'Women and the Professions in Germany 1930 to 1940' in A.J. Nicholls & E. Mathias (eds.), *German Democracy and the Triumph of Hitler* (London, 1971); J. Stephenson, *Women in Nazi Society* (London, 1975), pp. 116ff; H. Scholtz, *Nationalsozialistische Ausleseschulen* (Göttingen, 1973), pp. 132f, 145, 324ff; W.L. Bühl, *Schulaufbau und Bildungschancen in der Bundesrepublik Deutschland 1946-1966* (Stuttgart, 1970); M. Klewitz, *Berliner Einheitsschule 1945-1951* (Berlin, 1971); W. Fleischmann *et al.*, 'Materialien zum Problem der ökonomischen Implikationen von Schulreform in der BRD 1945-1970' in E. Altvater & F. Huisken, *Materialen zur politischen Ökonomie des Ausbildungssektors* (Erlangen, 1971).

9. See Table 3.2; Statistisches Bundesamt Wiesbaden (ed.), Facserie A: Bevölkerung und Kultur, Reihe 10, V, WS 1971/72, Stuttgart 1973 (Proportion of workers' children among freshmen 1971/72, which is used here as a substitute for the proportion of workers' children among all students which has not yet been published in this series); ibid., Hochschulbesuch. Ausgewählte Übersichten WS 1975/76, Stuttgart 1976.

10. W. Müller & K.U. Mayer, *Chancengleichheit durch Bildung? Untersuchungen über den Zusammenhang von Ausbildungsabschlüssen und Berufsstatus* (Stuttgart, 1976); see also, R. Rüge, 'Ziele und Ergebnisse der Bildungspolitik: Ansätze zu einem System von Bildungsindikatoren' in W. Zapf (ed.), *Lebensbedingungen in der Bundesrepublik* (Frankfurt, 1977).

11. It is, however, to be expected that comparative publications will soon become more frequent. In this connection, in addition to the plans for publication referred to in note 3 of this chapter, see P. Flora, *The HIEWED-Project: the Handbook, Theoretical Orientations and Statistical sources (HIWED report No. 1)* (Mannheim, 1975).

5. The Recruitment of Elites

1. See J.A. Armstrong, *The European Administrative Elite* (Princeton, 1973).

2. A. Schröter & W. Becker, *Die deutsche Maschinenindustrie in der industriellen Revolution* (Berlin, 1962), p. 65; C. Erickson, *British Industrialists. Steel and Hosiery 1850-1950* (Cambridge, 1959), pp. 79ff; P.L. Payne, *British Entrepreneurship in the 19th Century* (London, 1974), pp. 24ff; C. Wright Mills,

'The American Business Elite: A Collective Portrait', *Journal of Economic History*, 5 (1945), Supplement. (Mills's thesis depends to a large extent on whether one accepts his interpretation of farmers' sons as upwardly mobile since they provide the majority of those who were upwardly mobile during the industrial revolution. As Bendix and Howton demonstrate in the article referred to below, the majority of these fathers of businessmen at that particular period were big landowners, a family background that was undoubtedly very favourable from an economic point of view.) H.G. Gutman, 'The Reality of the Rag-to-Riches "Myth": The Case of the Paterson, New Jersey, Locomotive, Iron, and Machinery Manufacturers 1830-1880' in S. Thernstrom & R. Sennett (eds.), *Nineteenth-Century Cities* (New Haven/London 1969); cf. P.R. Decker, *Fortunes and Failures. White Collar Mobility in 19th Century San Francisco* (Cambridge, Mass., 1978).

3. R. Bendix & F.W. Howton, 'Social Mobility and the American Business Elite' in S.M. Lipset & R. Bendix (eds), *Social Mobility in Industrial Society* (Berkeley and Los Angeles 1963), pp. 121-8. (Bendix and Howton consider their source, the National Cyclopedia of American Biography, to be superior, since it was the first biographical dictionary to be concerned to record the business elite systematically, whereas Mills's source, the Dictionary of American Biography, often included businessmen who became well-known not as such but as politicians or who happened to have founded a business which only became really important under their successors, ibid., p. 119.) F.W. Gregory & I.D. Neu, 'The American Industrial Elite in the 1870s' in William Miller, (ed.), *Men in Business* (Cambridge, 1952), p. 202 (also for the textile and steel industries); R. Crandall, 'American Bankers in the 1970s', *Explorations in Entrepreneurial History*, 1st ser., 4, 1952/53; R. Crandall, 'American Railroad Presidents in the 1870s', ibid., 1949/50; J.N. Ingham, 'Rags to Riches Revisited: The Effect of City Size on the Recruitment of Business Leaders', *Journal of American History* (1976); see also a series of special studies: M. Klein, 'Southern Railroad Leaders, 1865-1893', *Business History Review*, 42 (1968); B.E. Supple, 'A Business Elite: German-Jewish Financiers in 19th Century New York', *Business History Review*, 31 (1957), pp. 144f, 149ff; H.R. Stevens, 'Bank Enterprisers in a Western Town, 1815-1822', *Business History Review*, 29 (1955), pp. 145ff; L.J. Arrington, 'Banking Enterprises in Utah, 1847-1880', *Business History Review*, 29 (1955), pp. 317ff; D.L. Kemmerer, 'Financing Illinois Industry 1880-1890', *Bulletin of the Business Historical Society*, 27 (1953), pp. 104ff.

4. Erickson, *British Industrialists*, pp. 11ff; T.R. Gourvish, 'A British Business Elite: The Chief Executive Managers of the Railway Industry 1850-1922', *Business History Review*, 47 (1973), pp. 291ff, 315f. See also, A. Birch, *An Economic History of the British Iron and Steel Industry 1784-1879* (London, 1967), pp. 276ff; S.D. Chapman, *The Early Factory Masters* (Newton Abbot, 1967), pp. 77ff; for further studies see H. Kaelble, *Berliner Unternehmer während der frühen Industrialisierung*, (Berlin, New York, 1972), pp. 115ff.

5. M. Lévy-Leboyer, 'Le Patronat francais a-t-il été malthusien?' *Le mouvement social*, 88 (1974), pp. 18ff; T. Zeldin, *France 1815-1945, vol. I: Ambition, Love and Politics* (Oxford, 1973), pp. 87ff; B. Gille, *La Sidérurgie francaise au XIXe siècle* (Geneva, 1968), pp. 16ff; C. Fohlen, *L'Industrie textile au temps du second empire* (Paris, 1956), pp. 67ff; J. Lambert Dansette, *Quelques familles du patronat textile de Lille-Armentières (1789-1914)* (Lille, 1954), pp. 308ff; G. Thuiller, 'Histoire bancaire régionale: en Nivernais de 1800 à 1880', in *Annales*, 10 (1955); B. Gille, *La Banque et le crédit en France de 1815 à 1848* (Paris, 1959), pp. 272ff; D.S. Landes, 'Vieille banque et banque nouvelle: la révolution financière du XIXe siècle', *Revue d'histoire moderne et contemporaine*, 3 (1956), p. 208; L. Bergeron, *Banquiers, négociants et manu-*

facturiers parisiens du Directoire à l'empire, 2 vols. (Paris, 1975); C. Charle, 'Les milieux d'affaires dans la structure de la classe dominante vers 1900',*Actes de la recherche*, nos. 20-21 (1978).

6. See W. Stahl, *Der Elitekreislauf in der Unternehmerschaft* (Frankfurt, 1973); H. Kaelble, 'Sozialer Aufstieg in Deutschland, 1850 bis 1914', *Vierteljahrschrift für Sozial- und Wirtschaftsgeschichte*, 60 (1973). The two analyses adopt in some respects different perspectives. Stahl's analysis also includes the Austrian and Swiss business elites, which are contained in the Neue Deutsche Biographie, arranges the businessmen according to the period of their birth, contrasts the eighteenth and nineteenth centuries and, in addition to the fathers' professions, also includes two other important aspects – religious denomination and geographical origin. My survey restricts itself to the business elite in the territory of the Germany of 1871, arranges the businessmen according to the period of their careers (1800-70; 1870-1914; 1918-33) and, for the sake of a limited comparison, only includes their fathers' occupations. Also the two analyses use slightly different occupational categories. Nevertheless, probably the most interesting figure, the proportion of businessmen whose fathers were themselves businessmen, is almost identical in both. For all categories of businessmen (founders, partners, heirs, executives) together, it was according to Stahl in the nineteenth century 56 per cent (estimated on the basis of Stahl, *Unternehmerschaft*, pp. 113, 120, 136, 139, 144, 147, 155, 158), in my survey 53-54 per cent (see Table 5.3); H. Beau, *Das Leistungswissen des frühindustriellen Unternehmers in Rheinland und Westfalen* (Köln, 1959), pp. 66ff; W. Huschke, *Forschungen über die Herkunft der thüringischen Unternehmer des 19. Jahrhunderts* (Baden-Baden, 1962); Kaelble, *Berliner Unternehmer* pp. 30ff; T. Pierenkemper, *Die westfälischen Schwerindustriellen 1852-1913* (Göttingen, 1978); Pierenkemper, Entrepreneurs in Heavy Industry: Upper Silesia and the Westphalian Region, 1852-1913', *Business History Review*, 53 (1979); R. Engelsing, 'Bremisches Unternehmertum', *Jahrbuch der Wittheit zu Bremen*, 2 (1958), pp. 50ff, 112; W. Fischer, 'Ansätze zur Industrialisierung in Baden 1770-1870', *Vierteljahrschrift für Sozial- und Wirtschaftsgeschichte*, 47 (1960), pp. 210ff; W. Zorn, *Handels- und Industriegeschichte Bayerisch-Schwabens 1648-1870* (Augsburg, 1961), pp. 208ff. For a whole series of local studies and an international comparison see Kaelble, *Berliner Unternehmer*, pp. 97-124; further developed in: H. Kaelble, 'Long-term Changes of the Recruitment of the Business Elite since the Industrial Revolution: Germany Compared to the US, Britain, and France', *Journal of Social History* (Spring, 1980), French version in M. Lévy-Leboyer (ed.), *Le Patronat de la seconde industrialisation* (Paris, 1979); H. Henning, *Sozialgeschichtliche Entwicklungen in Deutschland von 1815 bis 1860* (Paderborn, 1977).

7. J. Kocka, *Unternehmer in der deutschen Industrialisierung* (Göttingen, 1975), pp. 43-7 (English version, 'Entrepreneurs and Managers in German Industrialization', in P. Mathias & M.M. Postan, (eds.), *Cambridge Economic History of Europe*, vol. 7, part 1 (Cambridge, 1978)).

8. T.W. Acheson, 'Changing Social Origins of the Canadian Industrial Elite 1880-1910', *Business History Review*, 47 (1973); Mills, 'Business Elite', pp. 28ff; Payne, *British Entrepreneurship*, pp. 24ff; M.M. Postan, *An Economic History of Western Europe 1945-1964* (London, 1967), pp. 291ff.

9. Bendix & Howton, 'Business Elite', pp. 128-43; *The Big Business Executive/ 1964: A Study of His Social and Educational Background*, with the collaboration of M. Newcomer, (New York 1965), p. 32; J.H. Soltow, 'Origins of Small Business. Metal Fabricators and Machinery Makers in New England 1890-1957', *Transactions of the American Philosophical Society*, vol. 55, part 10 (1965), pp. 7, 11ff.

10. Erickson, *British Industrialists*, pp. 25ff, 188ff; R.V. Clements, *Managers*

(London, 1955), pp. 82ff. (Clements himself uses these figures very cautiously. They have two weaknesses: first, they exaggerate changes, since only the newly-appointed managers are included, not those already active; secondly up to 1925 the samples are very small. Thus Clements's data can only be used for 1930-55.) P. Stanworth & A. Giddens, 'An Economic Elite: A Demographic Profile of Company Chairmen' in P. Stanworth & A. Giddens (eds.), *Elites and Power in British Society* (London, 1974); H. Perkin, 'The Recruitment of Elites in British Society since 1880', unpublished MS, 1976, which the author kindly put at my disposal. For another version cf. Perkin, 'The Recruitment of Elites in British Society since 1880', *Journal of Social History* (Winter, 1980).

11. Lévy-Leboyer, 'Le patronat francais a-t-il été malthusien?' pp. 18ff; Lévy-Leboyer, *Innovation and business strategies in 19th and 20th century France* (Baltimore, 1976), pp. 104ff.

12. See H. Kaelble, 'Soziale Mobilität in Deutschland, 1900-1960', in H. Kaelble *et al., Probleme der Modernisierung in Deutschland* (Opladen, 1978); Kaelble, 'Social Mobility in Germany 1900-1960', *Journal of Modern History*, 50 (1978); Kaelble, 'Long-term Changes in the Recruitment of the Business Elite since the Industrial Revolution', *Journal of Social History* (Spring, 1980).

13. See A. Giddens, 'Elites in the British Class Structure', *Sociological Review*, 20 (1972).

14. W.L. Guttsman, *The British Political Elite* (New York, 1964); Guttsman, 'The British Political Elite and the Class Structure' in P. Stanworth & A. Giddens (eds.), *Elites and Power in British Society* (London, 1974); Guttsman, 'Elite Recruitment and Political Leadership in Britain and Germany since 1950: A Comparative Study of MPs and Cabinets' in I. Crewe (ed.), *Elites in Western Democracy. British Political Sociology Yearbook*, vol. I (London, 1974); P.G. Pulzer, *Political Representation and Elections in Britain,* 2nd edn (London, 1972), pp. 63ff, 156f; R.W. Johnson, 'The British Political Elite 1955-1972', *Archives européennes de sociologie*, 14 (1973); V.J. Hanby, 'A Changing Labour Elite: The National Executive Committee of the Labour Party 1900 to 1972' in I, Crewe (ed.), *Elites in Western Democracy, British Political Sociology Yearbook*, vol. 1 (London, 1974); H. Perkin, 'The Recruitment of Elites in British Society since 1880', unpublished MS; see, P.W. Buck, *Amateurs and Professionals in British Politics 1918-1959* (Chicago/London 1963) (without theories on the historical change in the recruitment of the political elite); J.F.S. Ross, *Elections and Electors* (London, 1955), pp. 404ff (further evidence for the above theories); J.A. Thomas, *The House of Commons 1906-1911: An Analysis of its Economic and Social Character* (Cardiff, 1958).

15. G. Chaussinand-Nogaret, Louis Bergeron & Robert Forster, 'Les notables du "Grand Empire" en 1810', *Annales*, 26 (1971); P.B. Higonnet, 'La composition de la chambre des députés de 1827 à 1831', *Revue historique*, 239 (1968); D.H. Pinkney, *The French Revolution of 1830* (Princeton, 1972), pp. 274ff; T.D. Beck, *French Legislators 1800 to 1834: a Study in Quantitative History* (Berkeley, 1974), pp. 108ff; M. Dogan, 'Les Filières de la carrière politique en France', *Revue française de sociologie*, 8 (1967); M. Dogan, 'Political Ascent in a Class Society: French Deputies 1870-1958', in D. Marwick (ed.), *Political Decision-Makers* (Glencoe, 1961); Jean Charlot, 'Les Élites politiques en France de la IIIe à la Ve république', *Archives européennes de sociologie*, 14 (1973); W. Giesselmann, *Die brumairianische Elite* (Stuttgart, 1977).

16. J.J. Sheehan, 'Political Leadership in the German Reichstag, 1871-1918', *American Historical Review*, 74 (1968); W. Zapf, *Wandlungen der deutschen Elite. Ein Zirkulationsmodell deutscher Führungsgruppen 1919-1961* (Munich, 1966); see also H. Brandt, 'Gesellschaft, Parlament und Regierung in Württemberg 1830-1840', in G.A. Ritter (ed.), *Gesellschaft, Parlament und Regierung* (Düsseldorf, 1974), pp. 106f.

17. D. Lerner, *The Nazi Elite* (Stanford, 1951), pp. 34ff, 84ff, 98f; M.E. Knight, *The German Executive 1890-1933* (Stanford, 1952), pp. 32ff; D. Schoenbaum, *Hitler's Social Revolution* (Garden City, 1967); W. Zapf, *Wandlungen der deutschen Elite*, pp. 38ff, 137ff, 168ff; R. Rogowski, 'The Gauleiter and the Social Origins of Fascism', *Comparative Studies in Society and History*, 19 (1977).

18. W.L. Guttsman 'Elite Recruitment and Political Leadership in Britain and Germany since 1950: A Comparative Study in MPs and Cabinets' in I. Crewe (ed.), *Elites in Western Democracy*.

6. Appendix: Concepts and Indicators

1. Most of the tables contain examples of historical comparisons, e.g. Tables 2.2, 2.3, 3.3 and 3.4.

2. Table 2.1 contains examples of cohort analyses. The best sociological discussion of cohort analysis: K.U. Mayer & W. Müller, 'Trendanalyse in der Mobilitätsforschung', *Kölner Zeitschrift für Soziologie*, 23 (1971); Revised version in: H. Kaelble (ed.), *Geschichte der sozialen Mobilität seit der industriellen Revolution* (Königstein, 1978). For a much more refined application of cohort analysis see Kaelble, 'Recent Developments in the Opportunity Structure of (West-) German Society 1955-1971', unpublished essay 1977.

3. N. Rogoff, *Recent Trends in Occupational Mobility* (Glencoe, 1953), pp. 29ff; Mayer & Müller, 'Trendanalyse'.

4. R. Boudon, *Mathematical Structures of Social Mobility* (London/New York, 1973).

5. C. Jencks, *Inequality*, (New York, 1973), appendix; W. Müller, 'Bildung und Mobilitätsprozess – eine Anwendung der Pfadanalyse', *Zeitschrift für Soziologie*, 1 (1972); Müller, *Familie, Schule, Beruf. Analysen zur Mobilität und Statuszuweisung in der Bundesrepublik* (Opladen 1975).

6. The first example of a historical path analysis was published when this research report had already gone to press: A.H. Halsey, 'Towards Meritocracy? The Case of Britain', in J. Karabel & A.H. Halsey (eds.), *Power and Ideology in Education* (New York, 1977), p. 183.

BIBLIOGRAPHY

1. Historical Theories and Research Surveys

Ammassari, P. 'Occupational Opportunity Structure in Advanced Society' in *Proceedings of the 1st Italo-Hungarian Meeting of Sociology* (Rome,1967)

Bolte, K.M. & Recker, H. 'Vertikale Mobilität' in R. König (ed.), *Handbuch der empirischen Sozialforschung*, 2nd edn, vol. 5 (Stuttgart, 1976)

Corbin, A. 'La mobilité sociale en France au 19e siècle', unpublished paper 1979 (to be published in the proceedings of the Franco-German meeting of historians 1979)

Dietrick, B.A. 'Social Mobility 1969-1973', *Annals of the American Academy of Political and Social Sciences*, 414 (1974)

Dupeux, G. 'L'Etude de la mobilité sociale. Quelques problèmes de méthodes' in *Conjoncture économique, structures sociales* (Paris, 1974)

Kaelble, H. (ed.) *Geschichte der sozialen Mobilität seit der industriellen Revolution* (Königstein, 1978)

Lipset, S.M. & Bendix, R. *Social Mobility in Industrial Society* (Berkeley, 1959)

Lipset, S.M. & Zetterberg, L. 'Eine Theorie der sozialen Mobilität'in B. Seidel & S. Jenkner (eds.), *Klassenbildung und Sozialschichtung* (Darmstadt, 1968)

Macdonald, K. & Ridge, J. 'Social mobility' in A.H. Halsey (ed.), *Trends in British Society since 1900* (London and New York, 1972)

Mayer, K.U. 'Soziale Mobilität' in E.R. Wiehn & K.U. Mayer (eds.), *Soziale Schichtung und Mobilität* (München, 1975)

Mendels, F.F. 'Social Mobility and Phases of Industrialization', *Journal of Interdisciplinary History*, 7 (1976)

Modell, J. 'Die Neue Sozialgeschichte in Amerika', *Geschichte und Gesellschaft*, 1 (1975)

Pessen, E. (ed.) *Three Centuries of Social Mobility in America* (Lexington, 1974)

Smelser, N.J. & Lipset, S.M. 'Social Structure, Mobility, and Development' in N.J. Smelser & S.M. Lipset (eds.), *Social Structure and Mobility in Economic Development* (London, 1966)

Sorokin, P.A. *Social and Cultural Mobility in Industrial Society* (Glencoe, 1959)

Svalastoga, K. *Prestige, Class and Mobility* (Copenhagen, 1959)

2. Studies of Countries and Cities

Akerman, S. 'Swedish Migration and Social Mobility: the Tale of Three Cities', *Social Science History* 1 (1977)

Aycoberry, P. 'Probleme der Sozialschichtung in Köln im Zeitalter der Frühindustrialisierung', in W. Fischer (ed.), *Wirtschafts- und sozial-geschichtliche Probleme der frühen Industrialisierung* (Berlin, 1968)

Barr, A. 'Occupational and Geographical Mobility in San Antonio, 1870-1900', *Social Science Quarterly*, 51 (1970)

Bertaux, D. 'Nouvelles perspectives sur la mobilité sociale en France', *Quality and Quantity*, 5 (1971)

Blau, P.M. and Duncan, O.D. *The American Occupational Structure* (New York, 1967)

Blumin, S. 'Mobility and Change in Ante-bellum Philadelphia', in S. Thernstrom & R. Sennet, (eds.), *Nineteenth Century Cities: Essays in the New Urban History* (New Haven London 1969)

Bodnar, J. *Immigration and Industrialization. Ethnicity in an American Mill Town, 1870-1940* (Pittsburgh, 1977)

Bolte, K.M. *Sozialer Aufstieg und Abstieg* (Stuttgart, 1959)

Carlsson, G. *Social Mobility and Class Structure* (Lund, 1958)

Chudacoff, H.P. *Mobile Americans. Residential and Social Mobility in Omaha, 1880-1920* (New York, 1972)

Daheim, H.J. 'Berufliche Intergenerationen-Mobilität in der komplexen Gesellschaft', *Kölner Zeitschrift für Soziologie und Sozialpsychologie*, 16 (1964)

Darbel, A. 'L'Evolution récente de la mobilité sociale', *Economie et Statistique*, 71 (1975)

Dijk. H. van 'De beroepsmobiliteit in Rotterdam in de negentiende eeuw', in J. van Herwaarden (ed.), *Lof der historie* (Rotterdam, 1974)

——— 'Sociaal-historisch onderzoek in Denmarken', *Tijdschrift voor Sociale Geschiedenis*, 1 (1976)

———*Rotterdam 1810-1880* (Schiedam, 1976)

Duncan, O.D. 'The Trend of Occupational Mobility in the United States', *American Sociological Review*, 30 (1965)

Esslinger, D.R. *Immigrants and the City. Ethnicity and mobility in a 19th-Century Midwestern Community* (Port Washington, 1975)

Fox. T. & Miller, M. 'Intra-Country Variations: Occupational Stratific-ication and Mobility', in R. Bendix & S.M. Lipset, *Class, Status and Power*, 2nd edn (New York, 1966)

Geiger, T. 'Soziale Umschichtungen in einer dänischen Mittelstadt', *Acta Jutlandica*, 23, 1 (Kopenhagen, 1951)

Glass, D.V. & Hall, J.R. 'Social Mobility in Great Britain: a Study of Inter-Generational Changes in Status' in: D.V. Glass (ed.), *Social Mobility in Britain* (London, 1954)

Goldstein, S. *Patterns of Mobility, 1910-1950: the Norristown study* (Philadelphia, 1958)

Goldthorpe, J.H., Llewellyn, J.H. & Payne, C. *Social Mobility and Class Structure in Modern Britain* (Oxford, 1980)

Goyder, J.C. & Curtis, J.E. 'A Three-Generational Approach to Trends in Occupational Mobility', *American Journal of Sociology*, 81 (1975)

Griffen, C. & Griffen, S. *Natives and Newcomers. The Ordering of Opportunity in Mid-Nineteenth-Century Poughkeepsie* (Cambridge, Mass., 1978)

Harris, A.J. & Clausen, R. *Labour Mobility in Great Britain, 1953-1963* (London, 1966)

Hauser, R.M. *et al.* 'Structural Changes in Occupational Mobility Among Men in the United States', *American Sociological Review*, 40 (1975)

—— 'Temporal changes in occupational mobility: evidence for men in US', ibid.

Hippel, W. 'Regionale und soziale Herkunft der Bevölkerung einer Industriestadt. Untersuchungen zu Ludwigshafen a. Rh. 1867-1914' in W. Conze & U. Engelhardt (eds.), *Arbeiter im Industrialisierungs-prozess* (Stuttgart, 1979)

Hofbauer, H. & Kraft, H. 'Materialien zur Statusmobilität bei männ-lichen Erwerbspersonen in der Bundesrepublik Deutschland', *Mitteil-ungen der Berufs- und Arbeitmarktforschung*, 5 (1972)

Hopkins, R.J. 'Occupational and Geographic Mobility in Atlanta, 1870-1896', *Journal of Southern History*, 34 (1968)

Jackson, E.F. & Crockett, H.J. 'Occupational Mobility in the United States: a Point Estimate and Trend Comparison', *American Socio-logical Review*, 29 (1964)

Kaelble, H. 'Sozialer Aufstieg in Deutschland 1850-1914', *Vierteljahrs-schrift für Sozial- und Wirtschaftsgeschichte*, 60 (1973). Also in K.H. Jarausch (ed.), *Quantifizierung in der Geschichtswissenschaft*(Düssel-dorf, 1976)

——— 'Sozialer Aufstieg in den USA and Deutschland, 1900-1960' in H.U. Wehler (ed.), *Sozialgeschichte Heute. Festschrift für Hans Rosenberg* (Göttingen, 1974)

——— 'Soziale Mobilität in Deutschland 1900-1960' in H. Kaelble *et al.* (eds.). *Probleme der Modernisierung in Deutschland* (Opladen, 1978)

——— 'Social mobility in Germany 1900-1960', *Journal of Modern History*, 50 (1978)

Katz, M.B. 'The People of a Canadian City: 1851-2', *Canadian Historical Review*, 53 (1972)

——— *The People of Hamilton, Canada West: Family and Class in a Mid-Nineteenth Century City* (Cambridge, Mass., 1975)

Kirk, G.W. & Kirk, C.T. 'Migration, Mobility, and the Transformation of the Occupational Structure in an Immigrant Community: Holland, Michigan, 1850-1880', *Journal of Social History*, 7 (1973/74)

Kleining, G. 'Struktur- und Prestigemobilität in der Bundesrepublik Deutschland', *Kölner Zeitschrift für Soziologie und Sozialpsychologie*, 23 (1971)

——— 'Die Veränderungen der Mobilitätschancen in der Bundesrepublik Deutschland', ibid.

——— 'Soziale Mobilität in der Bundesrepublik Deutschland, I: Klassenmobilität', ibid., 27 (1975)

——— 'Soziale Mobilität in der Bundesrepublik Deutschland, II: Status- oder Prestigemobilität', ibid., 27 (1975)

Knights, P.R. *The Plain People of Boston, 1830-1860. A Study in City Growth* (New York, 1972)

Kowalska, S. 'Ausgewählte Probleme der Sozialstrukturforschung', *Jahrbuch für Wirtschaftsgeschichte* (1970), III

Kreckel, R., Broek, D. & Thode, H. *Vertikale Mobilität und Immobilität in der Bundesrepublik Deutschland* (Bonn-Bad Godesberg, 1972)

Lenski, G.E. 'Trends in Inter-generational Occupational Mobility in the United States', *American Sociological Review*, 23 (1958)

Lipset, S.M. 'Social Mobility and Equal Opportunity', *Public Interest* (fall, 1972)

Marceau, J. 'Education and Social Mobility in France' in F. Parkin (ed.), *The Social Analysis of Class Structure* (London, 1974)

——— *Class Status in France. Economic Change and Social Immobility 1945-1975* (Oxford, 1977)

Mayer, K.U. & Müller, W. 'Progress in Social Mobility Research?', *Quality and Quantity*, 5 (1971)

—— 'Trendanalyse in der Mobilitätsforschung', *Kölner Zeitschrift für Soziologie und Sozialpsychologie*, 23 (1971)

—— 'Die Analyse von Mobilitätstrends', ibid., 24 (1972)

Mayntz, R. *Soziale Schichtung und sozialer Wandel in einer Industriegemeinde* (Stuttgart, 1958)

Michels, R. *Umschichtungen in den herrschenden Klassen nach dem Kriege* (Stuttgart, Berlin, 1934)

Milic, V. 'General Trends in Social Mobility in Yugoslavia', *Acta Sociologica*, 9 (1966)

Mukherjee, R. 'A Study of Social Mobility between Three Generations', in D.V. Glass (ed.), *Social Mobility in Great Britain* (London, 1954)

Ohngren, B. *Folk i rörelse* (Uppsala, 1974)

Pohl, R. *et al.* 'L'Enquête formation-qualification de 1970', *Les collections de l'INSEE*, vol. D32 (1974)

Pourcher, G. 'Un essai d'analyse par cohorte de la mobilité géographique et professionelle en France', *Acta Sociologica*, 9 (1965)

Praderie, M. & Passagez, M. 'La mobilité professionelle en France entre 1959 et 1964', *Etudes et Conjoncture*, 21 (1966) 10

Preston, B. *Occupations of Father and Son in Mid-Victorian England* (Reading, 1977)

Rishoy, T. 'Metropolitan Social Mobility 1850-1950. The case of Copenhagen', *Quality and Quantity*, 5 (1971)

—— 'Udviklingen af den sociale mobilitet id det storköbnhavnske omrade i periode 1850-1950', *Sociologiske meddelser*, 13 (1969)

Rogoff, N. *Recent Trends in Occupational Mobility* (Glencoe, 1953)

Schildt, G. 'Wachstum und Stagnation der sozialen Mobilität im 19. und 20. Jh', *Kölner Zeitschrift für Soziologie*, 29 (1977)

Schoenbaum, D. *Hitler's Social Revolution* (New York, 1967)

Sewell, W.H. 'Social Mobility in a Nineteenth Century European City', *Journal of Interdisciplinary History*, 7 (1976)

Stone, L. 'Social Mobility in England 1500-1700', *Past & Present*, 33 (1966)

Thernstrom, S. *The Other Bostonians* (Cambridge, Mass., 1973)

—— 'Immigrants and WASPs: Ethnic Differences in Occupational Mobility in Boston, 1890-1940' in S. Thernstrom & R. Sennet (eds.), *Nineteenth Century Cities* (New Haven, London, 1969)

—— 'Religion and Occupational Mobility in Boston 1880-1963' in W.O. Aydelotte (ed.), *The Dimensions of Quantitative Research in History* (Princeton 1972)

—— 'Urbanization, Migration and Social Mobility in late nineteenth century America' in B.J. Bernstein (ed.), *Toward a New Past:*

Dissenting Essays in American History (New York 1968)

—— 'Class and Mobility in a Nineteenth-Century City', in R. Bendix & S.M. Lipset (eds.), *Class, Status, and Power*, 2nd edn (New York, 1966)

Thernstrom, S. & Knights, P.R. 'Men in Motion: Some Data and Speculation about Urban Population Mobility in Nineteenth Century America' in T.K. Hareven (ed.), *History from the Bottom Up* (Englewood Cliffs 1970)

Tulder. J.J.M. van, *De beroepsmobiliteit in Nederland van 1919 tot 1954* (Leiden, 1952)

—— 'Occupational Mobility in the Netherlands from 1919 to 1954', in *Transactions of the Third World Congress of Sociology*, III (London, 1956)

Tully, J.C., Jackson, E.F. & Curtis, R.P. 'Trends in Occupational Mobility in Indianapolis', *Social Forces*, 49 (1970/71)

3. The Recruitment of Elites

3.1 General

Adams, S. 'Origins of American Occupational Elites, 1900-1955', *American Journal of Sociology*, 62 (1956/57)

Cecil, L.A. 'The Creation of Nobels in Prussia, 1871-1918', *American Historical Review*, 75 (1970)

Crewe, I. (ed.), *Elites in Western Democracy* (*British Political Sociology Yearbook*, 1) (London, 1974)

Daumard, A. *La Bourgeoisie Parisienne de 1815 à 1848* (Paris, 1963)

Giddens, A. 'Elites in the British Class Structure', *Sociological Review*, 20 (1972)

Girard, A. *La Réussite sociale en France* (Paris, 1961)

Harris, P.M.G. 'The Social Origin of American Leaders', *Perspectives in American History*, 3 (1969)

Henning, H.J. *Das westdeutsche Bürgertum in der Epoche der Hochindustrialisierung 1900-1914*, Part I (Wiesbaden, 1972)

Jaher, F.C. 'Nineteenth Century Elites in Boston and New York', *Journal of Social History*, 6 (1972/73)

Jannen, W. 'National Socialists and Social Mobility', *Journal of Social History*, 9 (1975/76)

Perkin, H. 'The Recruitment of Elites in British Society since 1880', *Journal of Social History* (winter, 1980)

Pessen, E. *Riches, Class and Power before the Civil War* (Lexington,

1973)

Shapiro, G. & Dawson, P. 'Social Mobility and Political Radicalism: the Case of the French Revolution of 1789', in W.O. Aydelotte *et al., The Dimension of Quantitative Research in History* (Princeton, 1972)

Sheehan, J.J. 'Conflict and Cohesion among German Elites in the 19th Century', in R.J. Bezucha (ed.), *Modern European Social History* (Lexington, 1972)

Stanworth, P. & Giddens, A. (eds.), *Elites and Power in British Society* (London, 1974)

Zapf, W. *Wandlungen der deutschen Elite*, 2nd edn (Munich, 1966)

3.2 Business Elites

Acheson, T.W. 'Changing Social Origins of the Canadian Industrial Elite 1880-1910', *Business History Review*, 47(1973)

Beau, H. *Das Leistungswissen des frühindustriellen Unternehmertums in Rheinland und Westfalen* (Cologne, 1959)

Bendix, R. & Howton, R.W. 'Social Mobility and the American Business Elite' in S.M. Lipset & R. Bendix, *Social Mobility in Industrial Society* (Berkeley, Los Angeles, 1963)

Bergeron, L. *Banquiers, negociants et manufacturiers parisiens du Directoire à l'Empire*, 2 vols. (Paris, 1975)

Bourdieu, P. & de Saint Martin, M. 'Le Patronat', *Actes de la recherche*, nos. 20-1 (1978)

Braun, R. *Sozialer und kultureller Wandel in einem ländlichen Industriegebiet (Zürcher Oberland) unter Einwirkung des Maschinen- und Fabrikwesens im 19. und 20. Jh* (Erlenbach, Zürich, Stuttgart, 1965)

Charle, C. 'Les milieux d'affaires dans la structure de la classe dominante vers 1900', *Actes de la recherche*, nos. 20-1 (1978)

Clements, R.V. *Managers. A Study of Their Careers in Industry* (London, 1958)

Decker, P.R. *Fortunes and Failures. White-collar Mobility in 19th Century San Francisco* (Cambridge, Mass., 1978)

Erickson, C. *British Industrialists. Steel and Hosiery 1850-1950* (Cambridge, 1959) (The National Institute of Economic and Social Research. Economic and Social Studies, 18)

Fischer, W. 'Ansätze zur Industrialisierung in Baden, 1770-1870', *Vierteljahrschrift für Sozial-und Wirtschaftsgeschichte*, 47 (1960)

Gille, B. *Recherches sur la formation de la grande enterprise capitaliste (1815-1848)* (Paris, 1959)

Gourvish, T.R. 'A British Business Elite: The Chief Executive Managers of the Railway Industry 1850-1922', *Business History Review*, 47 (1973)

Gregory, W. & Neu, I.D. 'The American Industrial Elite in the 1870s' in William Miller (ed.), *Men in Business* (Cambridge, 1952)

Gutman, H.G. 'The Reality of the Rag-To-Riches "Myth" ' in S. Thernstrom & R. Sennet (eds.), *Nineteenth-Century Cities* (New Haven, 1969)

Henning, H. 'Soziale Verflechtung der Unternehmer in Westfalen, 1860-1914', *Zeitschrift für Unternehmensgeschichte*, 1 (1978)

Ingham, J.N. 'Rags to Riches Revisited: the Effect of City Size on the Recruitment of Business Leaders', *Journal of American History* (1976)

—— *The Iron Barons: A Social Analysis of an American Urban Elite* (Westport, Conn., 1978)

Kaelble, H. *Berliner Unternehmer während der frühen Industrialisierung. Herkunft, sozialer Status und politischer Einfluss* (Berlin, New York, 1972)

—— 'Long-term Changes of the Recruitment of the Business Elite since the Industrial Revolution: Germany Compared to the US, Britain and France', *Journal of Social History* (spring, 1980)

Kocka, J. *Unternehmer in der deutschen Industrialisierung* (Göttingen, 1975)

Kocka, J. 'Entrepreneurs and Managers in German Industrialisation' in P. Mathias & M.M. Postan (eds.), *Cambridge Economic History of Europe*, 7, part 1, (Cambridge, 1978)

Kruk, M. *Die grossen Unternehmer* (Frankfurt, 1972)

Lambert Densette, J. *Quelques familles du patronat textile de Lille-Armentières (1789-1814). Origines et évolution d'une bourgeoisie* (Lille, 1954)

Lévy-Leboyer, M. 'Le Patronat français a-t-il été malthusien?', *Le mouvement social*, 88 (1974)

—— 'Innovation and Business Strategies in 19th and 20th-century France', in E.G. Carter *et al.*, *Enterprise and Entrepreneurs in 19th and 20th-century France* (Baltimore, 1976)

—— 'Le Patronat francais, 1912-1973', in M. Lévy-Leboyer (ed.), *Le Patronat de la seconde industrialisation*, (Paris, 1979)

Mills, C.W. 'The American Business Elite: a Collective Portrait', *Journal of Economic History*, 5 (1945) Supplement

Newcomer, M. *The Big Business Executive* (New York, 1955)

—— 'Professionalization of Leadership in the Big Business Corporation', *Business History Review*, 29 (1955)

Payne, P.L. *British Entrepreneurship in the 19th Century* (London, 1974)

Pross, H. & Bötticher, W. *Manager des Kapitalismus* (Frankfurt, 1971)

Pierenkemper, T. *Die westfälischen Schwerindustriellen 1852-1913* (Göttingen, 1978)

—— 'Entrepreneurs in Heavy Industry: Upper Silesia and the Westphalian Region, 1852-1913', *Business History Review*, 53 (1979)

Stahl, W. *Der Elitekreislauf in der Unternehmerschaft* (Frankfurt, 1973)

Stanworth, P. & Giddens, A. 'An Economic Elite: a Demographic Profile of Company Chairmen', in P. Stanworth & A. Giddens (eds.), *Elites and Power in British Society* (London, 1974)

Torstendahl, R. 'Les chefs d'entreprise en Suède de 1880 à 1950: sélection et milieu social', in M. Levy-Leboyer (ed.), *Le patronat dans la seconde industrialisation* (Paris, 1979)

—— *Dispersion of Engineers in a Transitional Society* (Uppsala, 1975)

Warner, W.L. & Abegglen, J.C. *Occupational Mobility in American Business and Industry* (Minneapolis, 1955)

Zapf, W. 'Die deutschen Manager. Sozialprofil und Karriereweg', in W. Zapf (ed.), *Beiträge zur Analyse der deutschen Oberschicht* (München, 1965)

3.3 Higher Civil Servants

Armstrong, J.A. *The European Administrative Elite* (Princeton, 1973)

Behrend, H.K. 'Zur Personalpolitik des preussischen Ministeriums des Innern. Die Besetzung der Landratsstellen in den östlichen Provinzen 1919-1933', *Jahrbuch für die Geschichte Mittel- und Ostdeutschlands*, 6 (1957)

Bendix, R. *Higher Civil Service in American Society* (Boulder, 1949)

Bottomore, T.B. 'Higher Civil Servants in France', in *Transactions of the Second World Congress of Sociology*, II (London, 1954)

—— 'La Mobilité sociale dans la haute administration française', *Cahiers Internationaux de Sociologie*, 13 (1952)

Bühler, H. *Das beamtete Bürgertum in Göppingen und sein soziales Verhalten* (Göppingen, 1976)

Chapman, R.A. *The Higher Civil Services in Britain* (London, 1970)

Demeter, K. *Das deutsche Offizierskorps in Gesellschaft und Staat 1650-1945* (Frankfurt, 1962)

Fenske, H. 'Preussische Beamtenpolitik vor 1918', *Staat*, 12 (1973)

—— 'Monarchisches Beamtentum und demokratischer Staat. Zum

Problem der Bürokratie in der Weimarer Republik' in *Demokratie und Verwaltung* (Berlin, 1972)

Ferrari, M. 'Origins and Careers in American Business, Government, and Academic Elites', *California Management Review*, 12 (1970)

Fry, G.K. *Statesmen in Disguise: The Changing Role of the Administrative Class of the British Home Civil Service, 1853-1966* (New York, 1969)

Gillis, J.R. 'Aristocracy and Bureaucracy in Nineteenth-Century Prussia', *Past & Present* 41 (1968)

—— *The Prussian Bureaucracy in Crisis, 1840-1860* (Stanford, 1971)

Gladden, E.N. *Civil Services of the United Kingdom, 1855-1970* (London, 1967)

Granick, D. *The European Executive* (Garden City, 1964)

Herwig, H.H. 'Zur Soziologie des kaiserlichen Seeoffizierskorps vor 1914' in H. Schottelius & W. Deist (eds.), *Marine und Marinepolitik im kaiserlichen Deutschland 1871-1914* (Düsseldorf, 1972)

Kelsall, R.K. 'The Social Background of Higher Civil Servants', in W.A. Robson (ed.), *The Civil Service in Britain and France* (London, 1956)

—— 'Recruitment to the Higher Civil Service: How has the Pattern Changed?' in P. Stanworth & A. Giddens (eds.), *Elites and Power in British Society* (London, 1974)

—— *Higher Civil Servants in Britain. From 1971 to the Present Day* (London, 1955)

Nightingale, R.T. 'The Personnel of the British Foreign Service and Diplomatic Service, 1851-1929', *American Political Science Review*, 24 (1930)

Otley, C.B. 'The Social Origins of British Army Officers', *Sociological Review*, 29 (1970)

Roehl, J.C.G. 'Higher Civil Servants in Germany 1890-1900', *Journal of Contemporary History*, 2 (1967)

Runge, W. *Politik und Beamtentum im Parteienstaat, 1918-1933* (Stuttgart, 1965)

Warner, W.L. *et al.*, *The American Federal Executive* (New Haven, 1963)

3.4 The Political Elite

Beck, T.D. *French Legislators 1800-1834. A study in Quantitative History* (Berkeley, 1974)

Buck, P.W. *Amateurs and Professionals in British Politics 1918-1959* (Chicago, London, 1963)

Charlot, J. 'Les Elites politiques en France de la III à la Ve république', *Archives européennes de sociologie*, 14 (1973)

Chaussinaud-Nogaret, C., Bergeron, L. & Forster, R. 'Les notables du "Grande Empire" en 1810', *Annales*, 26 (1971)

Deutsch, K.W. & Edinger, L.J. *Germany Rejoins the Powers* (Stanford, 1959)

Dogan, M. 'Political Ascent in a Class Society: French Deputies 1870-1958,' in D. Marwick (ed.), *Political Decision-Makers* (New York, 1961)

—— 'Les Filières de la carrière politique', *Revue française de sociologie*, 8 (1967)

—— 'L'Origine social du personnel parlamentaire française,' in M. Duverger (ed.), *Partis politiques et classes sociales* (Paris, 1955)

Dogan, M. & Scheffer von der Veen, M. 'Le Personnel ministerial hollandais: 1848-1958', *L'année sociologique* (1957/78)

Edinger, L.J. 'Continuity and Change in the Background of German Decision-Makers', *Western Political Quarterly*, 14 (1961)

—— 'Post-Totalitarian Leadership:Elites in the German Federal Republic', *American Political Science Review*, 54 (1960)

Gerth, H. 'The Nazi Party: its Leadership and Composition', *American Journal of Sociology*, 45 (1940)

Giesselmann, W. *Die brumairianische Elite. Kontinuität und Wandel der französischen Führungsschicht zwischen Ancien Régime und Julimonarchie* (Stuttgart, 1977)

Girard, L., Prost, A. & Gossez, R. *Les Conseillers généraux en 1870* (Paris, 1967)

Greaves, H.R.G. 'Personal Origins and Interrelations in the Houses of Parliament (since 1832)', *Economica*, 9 (1929)

Guttsman, W.L. 'Changes in British Labor Leadership' in D. Marwick, (ed.), *Political Decision-Makers* (New York, 1961)

—— *The British Political Elite* (New York, 1964)

—— 'The British Political Elite and the Class Structure,' in P. Stanworth & A. Giddens (eds.), *Elites and Power in British Society* (London, 1974)

—— 'Elite Recruitment and Political Leadership in Britain and Germany since 1950: A Comparative Study of MPs and Cabinets', in I. Crewe (ed.), *Elites in Western Democracy (British Political Sociology Yearbook, 1)* (London, 1974)

Hamon, L. 'Members of the French Parliament', *International Social Science Journal*, 13 (1952)

Hanby, V.J. 'A Changing Labour Elite: The National Executive Committee of the Labour Party 1900-1972', in I. Crewe (ed.), *Elites in Western Democracy (British Political Sociology Yearbook*, 1) (London, 1974)

Heinberg, J.G. 'Personnel of the French Cabinets', *American Political Science Review*, 25 (1931)

Higonnet, P.B. 'La Composition de la Chambre des Députés de 1827 à 1831', *Revue historique*, 239 (1968)

Johnson, R.W, 'The British Political Elite 1955-1972', *Archives européennes de sociologie*, 14 (1973)

Judd, G.F. *Members of Parliament, 1734-1832* (New Haven, 1955)

Kater, M. 'Sozialer Wandel in der NSDAP im Zuge der nationalsozialistischen Machtergreifung', in W. Schieder (ed.), *Faschismus als soziale Bewegung* (Hamburg, 1976)

—— 'Quantifizierung und NS-Geschichte. Methodologische Überlegungen über Grenzen und Möglichkeiten einer EDV-Analyse der NSDAP-Sozialstruktur von 1925 bis 1945', *Geschichte und Gesellschaft*, 3 (1977)

Knight, M.E. *The German Executive 1890-1933* (Stanford, 1952)

Laski, H.J. 'The Personnel of the English Cabinet 1801-1924', *American Political Science Review*, 22 (1928)

Lerner, D. *The Nazi Elite* (Stanford, 1951)

Pulzer, P.G.J. *Political Representation and Election in Britain*, 2nd edn (London, 1972)

Rogowski, R. 'The Gauleiter and the Social Origins of Fascism', *Comparative Studies in Society and History*, 19 (1977)

Ross, J.F.S. *Elections and Electors* (London, 1955)

Sartori, G. *Il parlamento italiano 1946-1963* (Napoli, 1963)

Schmidt, H. 'Die deutsche Exekutive 1949-1960', *Archives européennes de sociologie*, 4 (1963)

Schröder W.H. 'Probleme und Methoden von kollektiven Biographien. Das Beispiel der sozialdemokratischen Reichstagskandidaten (1898-1912)' in H. Best & R. Mann (eds.), *Quantitative Methoden in der historisch-sozialwissenschaftlichen Forschung* (Stuttgart, 1977)

Segal, D.R. 'Classes, Strata and Parties in West Germany and the United States', *Comparative Studies in Society and History*, 10 (1967/68)

Sheehan, J.J. 'Political Leadership in the German Reichstag, 1871-1918', *American Historical Review*, 74 (1968)

—— 'Quantification in the Study of Modern German Social and Political History', in V.R. Lorwin & J.M. Price (eds.), *The Dimension of the Past* (New Haven, 1972)

Thomas, J.A. *The House of Commons 1906-1911: An Analysis of its*

Economic and Social Character (Cardiff, 1958)

Whiteley, W.A. *The Social Composition of the British House of Commons 1868-1885* (London, 1970)

Willson, F.M.G. 'Some Career Patterns in British Politics: Whips in the House of Commons, 1906-1966', *Parliamentary Affairs*, 24 (1970)

―― 'Routes of Entry of New Members of the British Cabinet, 1801-1958', *Political Studies*, 18 (1970)

3.5 Professions

Berger, I. 'Sur l'origine de trois générations d'instituteurs et d'institutrices', *Bulletin de la Société d'études historiques, géographiques et scientifiques de la région parisienne*, 84 (1954)

Burger, A. 'Die Herkunft der Pfarrer nach Ausbildung und Beruf der Väter, verglichen mit den Theologiestudenten des Wintersemesters 1854/55', *Kirchliches Jahrbuch für die evangelische Kirche in Deutschland* (1955)

Duncan, O.D. 'Social Origins of Salaried and Self-Employed Professional Workers', *American Sociological Review*, 20 (1955)

Ferber, C. 'The Social Background of German University and College Professors since 1864,' *Transactions of the Third World Congress of Sociology*, III (London, 1956)

―― *Die Entwicklung des Lehrkörpers der deutschen Universitäten und Hochschulen 1864-1964* (Göttingen, 1956)

Floud, J. & Scott, W. 'Recruitment to Teaching in England and Wales', in A.H. Halsey *et al.* (eds.), *Education, Economy and Society* (Glencoe, 1961)

Halsey, A.H. & Trow, M. *The British Academics* (London, 1971)

McIntyre, J. 'Women and the Professions in Germany, 1930-1940', in A. Nicholls & E. Mathias (eds.), *German Democracy and the Triumph of Hitler* (London, 1971)

Rüschemeyer, D. *Lawyers and their Society* (Cambridge, Mass., 1973)

Stephenson, J. *Women in Nazi Society* (London, 1975)

West, S.S. 'Class Origins of Scientists', *Sociometry*, 24 (1961)

Sloczower, A. *Career Opportunities and the Growth of Scientific Discovery in 19th Century Germany* (Jerusalem, 1966)

4. Social Ascent of Workers

Anderson, M. *Family Structure in 19th Century Lancashire* (Cambridge, 1971)

Borscheid, P. & Schomerus, H. 'Mobilität und soziale Lage der württembergischen Fabrikarbeiterschaft im 19. Jahrhundert', in P.J. Miller (ed.), *Die Analyse prozess-orientierter Daten* (Stuttgart, 1977) —— *Textilarbeiterschaft in der Industrialisierung* (Stuttgart, 1978)

Chassagne, S., Dewerpe, A. & Gaulupeau, Y. 'Les ouvriers de la manufacture de toiles imprimées d'Oberkampf à Jouy-en-Josas (1760-1815)', *Le Mouvement social*, 97 (1976)

Crew, D. 'Definitions of Modernity: Social Mobility in German Town, 1880-1901', *Journal of Social History*, 7 (1973) —— 'Regionale Mobilität und Arbeiterklasse, Das Beispiel Bochum', *Geschichte und Gesellschaft*, 1 (1975) —— *Town in the Ruhr. A Social History of Bochum, 1860-1914* (New York, 1979)

Crossick, G. 'The Labour Aristocracy and its Values: A Study of Mid-Victorian Kentish London, *Victorian Studies*, 19 (1976) —— *An Artisan Elite in Victorian Society. Kentish London 1840-1880*, (London, 1978)

Dawley, A. *Class and Community* (Cambridge, 1976)

Engelsing, R. *Zur Sozialgeschichte der Mittel- und Unterschichten*, 2nd edn (Göttingen, 1978)

Eriksson, I. & Rogers, J. *Rural Labor and Population Change. Social and Demographic Developments in East-Central Sweden in the 19th Century* (Uppsala, 1978)

Gitelman, H.G. *Working Men of Waltham. Mobility in American Urban Industrial Development 1850-1890* (Baltimore, London, 1974)

Gray, R.Q. 'Thrift and Working Class Mobility in Victorian Edinburgh' in A. MacLaren (ed.), *Social Class in Scotland* (Edinburgh, 1976)

Griffen, C. 'Making it in America: Social Mobility in Mid-Nineteenth Century Poughkeepsie, *New York History*, 51 (1970) —— 'Workers Divided: The Effect of Craft and Ethnic Differences in Poughkeepsie', New York 1850-1880' in S. Thernstrom & R. Sennet (eds.), *Nineteenth Century Cities* (New Haven, London, 1969)

Hardach, G. *Der soziale Status des Arbeiters in der Frühindustrialisierung. Eine Untersuchung über die Arbeitnehmer in der französischen eisenschaffenden Stahlindustrie zwischen 1800 und 1870* (Berlin, 1969)

Hobsbawm, E.J. 'The Labor Aristocracy in Nineteenth-Century Britain' in P.W. Stearns & D. Walkowitz (eds.), *Workers in the Industrial Revolution* (New Brunswick, 1974)

Kearns, D.T. 'The Social Mobility of New Orleans Laborers, 1870-1900' (unpublished PhD thesis, Tulane University, 1977)

Kocka, J. 'The Study of Social Mobility and the Formation of the Working Class in the 19th Century', *Le mouvement social* (forthcoming)

Lequin, Y. 'La formation du prolétariat industriel dans la région lyonnaise au XIXe siècle', *Le mouvement social*, 97 (1976)

—— *Les ouvriers de la région lyonnaise dans la seconde moitié du XIXe siècle, 1848-1914. D'un monde ouvrier à la classe ouvrière* (Lyon, 1977)

Marquardt, F.D. 'Sozialer Aufstieg, sozialer Abstieg und die Entstehung der Berliner Arbeiterklasse, 1806-1848', *Geschichte und Gesellschaft*, 1 (1975)

McBride, T. 'Social Mobility for the Lower Class: Domestic Servants in France', *Journal of Social History* (fall, 1974)

—— *The Domestic Revolution: The Modernization of Household Service in England and France 1820-1920* (London, 1976)

Niethammer, L. 'Wie wohnen die Arbeiter im Kaiserreich?' *Archiv für Sozialgeschichte*, 16 (1977)

Rupieper, H.-J. 'Regionale Herkunft, Fluktuation und innerbetriebliche Mobilität der Arbeiterschaft der Maschinenfabrik Augsburg-Nürnberg 1844-1914' in W. Conze & U. Engelhardt (eds.), *Arbeiter im Industrialisierungsprozess* (Stuttgart, 1979)

Sanderson, M. 'Literacy and Social Mobility in the Industrial Revolution', *Past & Present*, 56 (1972)

—— 'Education and the Factory in Industrial Lancashire, 1780-1840', *Economic History Review*, 20 (1967)

Schomerus, H. 'Ausbildung und Aufstiegsmöglichkeiten württembergischer Metallarbeiter 1850 bis 1914 am Beispiel der Maschinenfabrik Esslingen' in U. Engelhardt, V. Sellin & E. Stuke (eds.), *Soziale Bewegung und politische Verfassung* (Stuttgart, 1976)

—— *Die Arbeiter der Maschinenfabrik Esslingen. Forschungen zur Lage der Arbeiterschaft im 19. Jahrhundert* (Stuttgart, 1977)

—— 'Saisonarbeit und Fluktuation. Überlegungen zur Struktur der mobilen Arbeiterschaft 1850-1914' in W. Conze & U. Engelhardt (eds.), *Arbeiter im Industrialisierungsprozess* (Stuttgart, 1979)

Scott, J.W. *The Glassworkers of Carmaux* (Cambridge, 1974)

—— 'The glassworkers of Carmaux 1850-1900' in S. Thernstrom & R. Sennett (eds.), *Nineteenth-Century Cities* (New Haven, London, 1969)

Sewell, W.H. 'The Working Class of Marseille under the Second Republic: Social Structure and Political behaviour' in P.N. Stearns & J. Walkowitz (eds.), *Workers in the Industrial Revolution: Recent*

Studies of Labor in the United States and Europe (New Brunswick, 1974)

—— 'Social Mobility in a Nineteenth Century European City: Some Findings and Implications', *Journal of Interdisciplinary History*, 7 (1976)

Stearns, P.N. 'Adaption to Industrialization: German Workers as a Test Case', *Central European History*, 3 (1970)

—— *Lives of Labour* (London, 1975)

Tenfelde, K. *Sozialgeschichte der Bergarbeiterschaft an der Ruhr im 19. Jahrhundert* (Bonn-Bad Godesberg, 1977)

—— 'Bildung und sozialer Aufstieg im Ruhrbergbau vor 1914' in W. Conze & U. Engelhardt (eds.), *Arbeiter im Industrialisierungsprozess* (Stuttgart, 1979)

Thernstrom, S. 'Working-Class Social Mobility in Industrial America' in M. Richter (ed.), *Essays in Theory and History* (Cambridge, 1970)

—— 'Class and Mobility in a Nineteenth-Century City' in R. Bendix & S.M. Lipset (eds.), *Class, status and power*, 2nd edn (New York, 1966)

—— *Poverty and Progress: Social Mobility in a Nineteenth-Century City* (Cambridge, 1964)

Trempé, R. *Les Mineurs de Carmaux, 1848-1914*, 2 vols. (Paris, 1971)

Woronoff, D. 'Le Monde ouvrier de la sidérurgie ancienne: note sur l'exemple français', *Le mouvement social*, 97 (1976)

Worthman, P.B. 'Working Class Mobility in Birmingham, Alabama, 1880-1914' in T.K. Hareven (ed.), *Anonymous Americans* (Englewood Cliffs, 1971)

Zwahr, H. *Zur Konstituierung des Proletariats als Klasse. Strukturuntersuchungen über das Leipziger Proletariat während der industriellen Revolution* (Berlin, 1978)

5. Recruitment of Lower Middle Class

Bongartz, W. 'Fachschulausbildung als Weg sozialen Aufstiegs für Fabrikarbeiter des Hüttenwesens und des Maschinenbaus am Beispiel von Betriebsangehörigen der GHH (1882-1914)', *Zeitschrift für Unternehmensgeschichte*, 1 (1978)

Crossick, G. 'The Emergence of the Lower Middle Class in Britain' in G. Crossick (ed.), *The Lower Middle Class in Britain 1870-1914* (London, 1977)

Faure, A. 'L'épicerie parisienne au XIXe siècle ou la corporation éclatée', *Le mouvement social*, 108 (1979)

Glovka-Spencer, E. 'Between Capital and Labor: Supervisory Personnel in Ruhr Heavy Industry before 1914', *Journal of Social History*, 9 (1975)

Henning, H.J. *Das westdeutsche Bürgertum in der Epoche der Hochindustrialisierung 1860-1914*, Part 1 (Wiesbaden, 1972)

—— *Sozialgeschichtliche Entwicklungen in Deutschland von 1815-1860* (Paderborn, 1977)

Kaelble, H. 'Soziale Mobilität in Deutschland 1900-1960' in H. Kaelble, H. Matzerath, H.-J. Rupieper, P. Steinbach & H. Volkmann, *Probleme der Modernisierung in Deutschland. Sozialgeschichtliche Studien zum 19. und 20. Jahrhundert* (Opladen, 1978)

Kocka, J. 'Industrielle Angestelltenschaft in frühindustrieller Zeit', in O. Büsch (ed.), *Untersuchungen zur Geschichte der frühen Industrialisierung vornehmlich im Wirtschaftsraum Berlin/Brandenburg* (Berlin, 1971)

——*Angestellte zwischen Faschismus und Demokratie. Zur politischen Sozialgeschichte der Angestellten: USA 1890-1940 im internationalen Vergleich* (Göttingen, 1977)

—— 'Bildung, soziale Schichtung und soziale Mobilität im deutschen Kaiserreich am Beispiel der gewerblich-technischen Ausbildung' in B.J. Wendt, D. Stegmann & P.C. Witt (eds), *Industrielle Gesellschaft und politisches System* (Bonn, 1978)

La Yaouanq, J. 'La Mobilité sociale dans le milieu boutiquier parisien au 19e siècle: Traitement d'un échantillon de trois generations', *Le mouvement social*, 108 (1979)

Lundgreen, P. *Techniker in Preussen während der frühen Industrialisierung* (Berlin, 1975)

Mayer, A.J, 'The Lower Middle Class as a Historical Problem', *Journal of Modern History*, 47 (1975)

Speier, H. *Die Angestellten vor dem Nationalsozialismus. Ein Beitrag zum Verständnis der deutschen Sozialstruktur 1918-1933* (Göttingen, 1977)

Steiner, H. *Soziale Strukturveränderungen im modernen Kapitalismus. Zur Klassenanalyse der Angestellten in Westdeutschland* (Berlin, 1967)

Torstendahl, R. *Dispersion of Engineers in a Transitional Society. Swedish Technicians 1860-1940* (Uppsala, 1976)

6. Educational Opportunities

Anderson, C.A. 'Access to Higher Education and Economic Development' in A.H. Halsey, J. Floud & C.A. Anderson (eds.), *Education, Economy and Society* (New York, 1965)

Anderson C.A. & Schnaper, M. *School and Society in England. Social Background of Oxford and Cambridge Students* (Washington, 1952)

Anderson, R. 'The Conflict in Education. Catholic Secondary Schools 1850-1870: A Reappraisal' in T. Zeldin (ed.), *Conflicts in French Society* (London, 1970)

—— *Education in France 1848-1870* (Oxford, 1975)

—— 'Secondary Education in Mid-Nineteenth Century France: Some Social Aspects', *Past & Present*, 53 (1971)

Bamford, T.W. 'Public Schools and Social Class 1801-1850', *British Journal of Sociology*, 12 (1961)

Barbagli, M. *Disoccupazione intelletuale e sistema scholastico in Italia (1859-1973)* (Bologna, 1974)

Boudon, R. *Education, Opportunity and Social Inequality. Changing Prospects in Western Society* (New York, 1973)

Bühl, W.I. *Schulaufbau und Verteilung der Bildungschancen in der Bundesrepublik Deutschland (1925-1960)* (München, 1965)

Chisick, H. 'Bourses d'études et mobilité sociale en France à la veille de la révolution', *Annales*, 30 (1975)

Conrad, J. *Das Universitätsstudium in Deutschland während der letzten 50 Jahre* (Jena, 1884)

Daheim, H.J. 'Soziale Herkunft, Schule und Rekrutierung der Berufe' in D.V. Glass & R. König (eds.), *Soziale Schichtung und soziale Mobilität*, 3rd edn (Köln, Opladen, 1968) (*Kölner Zeitschrift für Soziologie und Sozialpsychologie*, Sonderheft 5)

Daumard, A. 'Les Elèves de l'école polytechnique de 1815 à 1848', *Revue d'histoire moderne et contemporaine*, 5 (1958)

Day, C.R. 'Technical and Professional Education in France: The Rise and Fall of l'Enseignement Secondaire Spécial, 1865-1902', *Journal of Social History*, 6 (1973/4)

Duncan, O.D., Featherman, L. & Duncan, B. *Socioeconomic Background and achievement* (New York, London, 1972)

Floud, J. 'Der Einfluss schichtspezifischer Faktoren auf den Schulerfolg' in H.P. Widmaier (ed.), *Begabung und Bildungschancen* (Frankfurt, 1967)

—— 'The Educational Experience of Adult Population in England and Wales' in D.V. Glass (ed.), *Social Mobility in Britain* (London, 1954)

—— 'Social Class Factors in Educational Achievement' in M. Craft (ed.), *Family, Class and Education* (London, 1970). Also in A.H. Halsey (ed.), *Ability and Educational Opportunity* (Paris, 1961)

Floud, J., Halsey, A.H. & Martin, F.M. *Social Class and Educational Opportunity* (London, 1972)

Frijhoff, W. & Julia, D. *Ecole et société dans la France d'ancien régime* (Paris, 1975)

Girard, A. 'Die sozialen Bedingungen für Ausbildung und Aufstieg in Frankreich' in D.V. Glass & R. König (eds.), *Soziale Schichtung und soziale Mobilität*, 3rd edn (Köln, Opladen, 1968)

Halsey, A.H. 'Towards meritocracy? The Case of Britain' in J. Karabel & A.H. Halsey (eds.), *Power and Ideology in Education* (New York, 1977)

Harrigan, P.J. 'Secondary Education and the Professions in France during the Second Empire', *Comparative Studies in Society and History*, 17 (1975)

—— 'The Social Origins, Ambitions and Occupations of Secondary Students in France during the Second Empire' in L. Stone (ed.), *Schooling and Society: Studies in the History of Education* (Baltimore, 1976)

Heidenheimer, A.J. & Parkinson, M. 'Equalizing Educational Opportunity in Britain and the United States' in W.E. Gwyn & G. Edwards (eds.), *Perspectives on Public Policy Making* (New Orleans, (1975)

—— 'The Politics of Educational Reform. Explaining Different Outcomes of School Comprehensivization in Sweden and West Germany', *Comparative Education Review*, 18 (1974)

Herrlitz, H.G. & Titze, H. 'Überfüllung als bildungspolitische Strategie. Zur administrativen Steuerung der Lehrerarbeitslosigkeit in Preussen 1870-1914' in U. Hermann (ed.), *Schule und Gesellschaft im 19. Jahrhundert* (Weinheim, 1977)

Hermann, U. (ed.) *Schule und Gesellschaft im 19. Jahrhundert* (Weinheim, 1977)

Hurn, C.J. 'Recent Trends in the Sociology of Education in Britain', *Harvard Educational Review*, 46 (1976)

Jarausch, K.H. 'The sources of German Student Unrest 1815-1848' in L. Stone (ed.), *The University in Society*, vol. 2 (Princeton, 1974)

—— 'Die neuhumanistische Universität und die bürgerliche Gesellschaft 1800-1870', *Vierteljahrschrift für Sozial- und Wirtschaftsgeschichte* (1978)

—— 'The Social Transformation of the University in the Case of Prussia 1865-1914', *Journal of Social History*, 12 (1979/80)

Jencks, C. & Riesman, D. *The Academic Revolution* (Garden City, 1968)

Jenkins, H. & Jones, D.C. 'Social Class of Cambridge University Alumni of the 18th and 19th Centuries', *British Journal of Sociology*, 1 (1950)

Kaelble, H. 'Chancenungleichheit und akademische Ausbildung, 1910-1960', *Geschichte und Gesellschaft*, 1 (1975)

—— 'Educational Opportunities and Government Policies: Post-Primary European Education before 1914' in P. Flora & A. Heidenheimer (eds.), *The Development of the Welfare State in Europe* (New Brunswick, 1980)

Kaestle, C.F. *The Evolution of an Urban School System* (Cambridge, 1973)

Karady, V. 'L'Expansion universitaire et l'évolution des inégalités devant la carrière d'enseignant au début de la IIIe république', *Revue française de sociologie*, 14 (1973)

Kater, M.H. *Studentenschaft und Rechtsradikalismus in Deutschland 1918-1933* (Hamburg, 1975)

Kelsall, R.K. 'Self-Recruitment in Four Professions' in D.V. Glass (ed.), *Social Mobility in Britain* (London, 1954)

Kocka, J. 'Bildung, soziale Schichtung und soziale Mobilität im deutschen Kaiserreich am Beispiel der gewerblich-technischen Ausbildung' in B.J. Wendt & D. Stegmann (eds.), *Industrielle Gesellschaft und politisches System* (Bonn, 1978)

Koppenhöfer, P. 'Höhere Bildung und Auslese, Untersuchungen zur sozialen Herkunft der höheren Schulen Badens 1834/36-1890' (PhD thesis, Heidelburg, 1977)

Kraul, M. 'Untersuchungen zur sozialen Struktur der Schülerschaft des preussischen Gymnasiums im Vormärz', *Bildung und Erziehung*, 29 (1976)

—— *Gymnasium und Gesellschaft im Vormärz* (Göttingen, 1980)

Kuhlmann, C. *Schulreform und Gesellschaft in der Bundesrepublik 1946-1966* (Stuttgart, 1970). Also in S.B. Robinson (ed.), *Schulreform im gesellschaftlichen Prozess*, vol. 1 (Stuttgart, 1970)

Little, A. & Westergaard, J. 'The Trend of Class Differentials in Educational Opportunity in England and Wales', *British Journal of Sociology*, 15 (1964)

Lundgreen, P. 'Von der Gesamtschule zum sozialen Klassenschulsystem und zu einer Reduzierung der Bildungschancen? Überlegungen zur Reichweite und Interpretationsmöglichkeit schulgeschichtlicher Befunde anlässlich des Buches "Sozialstruktur und Schulsytem" von

D.K. Müller', *Zeitschrift für Pädagogik*, 24 (1978)

—— 'Historische Bildungsforschung' in Rürup (ed.), *Historische Sozial-wissenschaft* (Göttingen, 1977)

Mathew, M. 'The Origins and Occupations of Glasgow Students, 1740-1839', *Past & Present*, 33 (1966)

Milberg, H. *Schulpolitik in der pluralistischen Gesellschaft. Die politischen und sozialen Aspekte der Schulreformen in Hamburg 1890-1935* (Hamburg, 1975)

Müller, D.K. *Sozialstrukture und Schulsysteme. Aspekte zum Strukturwandel des Schulwesens im 19. Jahrhundert* (Göttingen, 1977)

—— 'Sozialstruktur und Schulsystem — Forschungsbericht über eine mehrdimensionale Analyse des Schulwesens im 19. Jahrhundert. Modellfall Berlin' in W. Rüegg & O. Neuloh (eds.), *Zur soziologischen Theorie und Analyse des 19. Jh.* (Göttingen, 1971)

Müller, W. 'Bildung und Mobilitätsprozess — eine Anwendung der Pfadanalyse', *Zeitschrift für Soziologie*, 1 (1972)

Müller, W. & Mayer, K.U. *Chancengleichheit durch Bildung. Untersuchungen über den Zusammenhang von Ausbildungsabschlüssen und Berufsstatus* (Stuttgart, 1976)

Nilsson, A. 'Study Financing and Expansion of Education', *Economy and History*, 20 (1977)

O'Boyle, L. 'Klassische Bildung und soziale Struktur in Deutschland zwischen 1800-1848', *Historische Zeitschrift*, 207 (1968)

Peyre, C. 'L'Origine sociale des élèves de l'enseignement secondaire en France' in P. Naville (ed.), *Ecole et société* (Paris, 1958)

Ridge, J.M. 'Fathers and sons' in J.M. Ridge (ed.), *Mobility in Britain Reconsidered* (Oxford, 1974)

Ringer, F.K. 'Higher Education in Germany in the Nineteenth Century', *Journal of Contemporary History*, 2 (1967)

—— *Education and Society* (Bloomington, 1979)

—— 'The Education of Elites in Modern Europe', *History of Education Quarterly*, 18 (1978)

Rothblatt, S. *The Revolution of the Dons: Cambridge and Society in Victorian England* (London, 1968)

Sanderson, M. 'Literacy and Social Mobility in the Industrial Revolution', *Past & Present*, 56 (1972)

Simon, B. *Studies in the History of Education 1780-1870* (London, 1960)

Stone, L, 'The Size and Composition of the Oxford Student Body 1580-1910' in L. Stohe (ed.), *The University in Society*, vol. 1 (Princeton, 1974)

Titze, H. *Die Politisierung der Erziehung* (Frankfurt, 1973)

Trow, M. 'The Democratization of Higher Education in America', *European Journal of Sociology*, 3 (1962)

—— 'The Second Transformation of American Secondary Education' in J. Karabel & A.H. Halsey (eds.), *Power and Ideology in Education* (New York, 1977)

Westergaard, J. & Little, A. 'Educational Opportunity and Social Selection in England and Wales. Trends and Policy Implications' in M. Craft (ed.), *Family, Class and Education* (London, 1970)

Zorn, W. 'Hochschule und höhere Schule in der deutschen Sozialgeschichte der Neuzeit' in K. Repgen & S. Skalweit (eds.), *Spiegel der Geschichte, Festgabe Braubach* (Münster, 1961)

INDEX

160 *Index*